The Spirit of Liberty

The Founding Fathers'
Message to America
and Your Role in It

By Suzanne Freeman

spring creek
BOOK COMPANY

ISBN 13: 978-1-932898-94-1
e. 1

Published by:
Spring Creek Book Company
www.springcreekbooks.com

Edited by Elizabeth Cheever

Cover design © Spring Creek Book Company
Printed in the United States of America
Printed on acid-free paper

DEDICATION

To Father in Heaven, the Lord Jesus Christ,
and to all of the Patriots: past, present, and future.

ACKNOWLEDGMENTS

To my family, my publisher who believes in me, and also to my sweet sister at heart, Elizabeth Cheever, who so tirelessly edited my thoughts and feelings to shape this book.

I also appreciate all those friends who inspired and encouraged me throughout the writing of this book.

Some had to use tough-love by saying, "Get over yourself and just write it, because it's not about you."

To all these I say, "Thank you, and I love you with all my heart."

Table of Contents

FOREWORD

by Chad Daybell
Author of the Standing in Holy Places *series*

It has been a great privilege to work with Suzanne Freeman throughout the years. She is a wonderful person, and I wanted to share some background on how her books came to fruition.

Prior to establishing Spring Creek Book Company in 2004, I had worked as the managing editor for a company that published a variety of books, including some by authors who claimed to have had supernatural experiences.

As I would meet with these authors, I became fairly good at determining whether they were being completely honest, or whether their stories had been "spruced up" with fantastic details in order to sell books. Quite often their accounts just didn't ring true. I became very cautious in selecting manuscripts from this genre for publication.

So as I embarked on my new publishing venture, I vowed to avoid the supernatural realm. However, less than a year later an author named Shirley Bahlmann called me. She had been approached at a book signing by a woman named Suzanne Freeman, who claimed to have died, gone to the Spirit World, and then returned to her body. Suzanne said she was feeling prompted to share her experience with people on a larger scale, even though she was a shy person and was very reluctant to do so.

Shirley invited Suzanne to her home, where she took some notes and came away impressed by Suzanne's account. She soon called me to say I should talk with Suzanne to see whether I would be interested in publishing it. I felt some hesitation based on my previous experiences, but I had worked with Shirley before and I trusted her judgment.

Less than a week later I made the drive to Ephraim, Utah and entered Shirley's front room, where I first met Suzanne. She stood up and shook my hand, and although I sensed she was nervous, my first impression was, "Wow, she actually seems normal!" She hadn't donned a fancy dress to impress me, but was just wearing a blouse and jeans.

Shirley was cooking something in the kitchen, so she excused herself and left us to discuss Suzanne's experience. As Shirley left the room, Suzanne said, "I'm not sure where to begin."

"That's okay," I said. "Please just tell me what happened when you crossed to the other side."

She started by giving me a brief synopsis of her near-death experience, and when she finished I asked her if she'd read other near-death accounts, wondering if she had "borrowed" some ideas from those stories.

She shook her head, explaining that she was a housewife with several children that occupied nearly all of her time. She was familiar with the basic truths of her Christian religion, but she said she certainly wasn't a gospel scholar. She even mentioned she'd had dyslexia as a child and that reading still didn't come easily to her.

I was feeling quite confident Suzanne was telling me the truth—that a humble housewife from a small Utah town had actually died, met the Savior, and returned. However, before I'd even consider publishing her story, I wanted to make sure her account stayed consistent within itself.

I began asking her many questions to see if she would slip up or change her story, but throughout the "interrogation" she looked me in the eyes and was straightforward with her answers.

After about thirty minutes, I felt satisfied and said, "I believe you. I feel we should publish your experience."

Suzanne seemed uncertain whether she had heard me correctly. "Really?" she asked. "You believe me?"

She then explained she'd been ridiculed within her family and in her community for even mentioning her experience, and she'd expected the same outcome from our meeting. I assured her that I believed her.

Shirley had rejoined us in the front room, and she agreed to help write the book. Within a few months *Led by the Hand of Christ* was published, which told of Suzanne's various experiences while in the Spirit World, including meeting some of the Founding Fathers of the United States.

While she was in the Spirit World, Suzanne had also been shown a series of troubling future world events. At first I pushed Suzanne to include these events in her book, but even talking about them caused her great distress, so I backed off. I sensed she had been shown those events for a reason, but that possibly the time hadn't yet come for her to share them.

We were pleased when *Led by the Hand of Christ* sold well throughout 2005, and Suzanne spoke to several groups about her experience. As the months passed, she felt more comfortable with describing the future events she had been shown by the Savior. She collaborated again with Shirley in sharing what she had seen, and *Through the Window of Life* was released in 2006.

This second book told of troubling times America would soon face, and although the book sold well, it was greeted with skepticism by many readers. They couldn't fathom that such problems could be coming to America. At that time, the nation's economy was humming along as the stock market soared. Subprime mortgages were fueling the housing market, and unemployment numbers were low. The Iraqi leader Saddam Hussein had been put to death, and America was seemingly on top of the world. What could possibly go wrong?

So by early 2007, Suzanne's book sales were slowing down, along with her invitations for speaking engagements. She had never sought the spotlight, so this was fine with her. She felt she had fulfilled the Savior's request to share her message, and now she could fully focus again on raising her family.

During this time, I was writing the *Standing in Holy Places* series. These five novels are in many ways a fictionalized version of the future events Suzanne had seen. As I finished the series' final novel in early 2011, I felt impressed that I should include the first chapter of *Through the Window of Life* as a bonus at the end of that volume. I explained to the readers that Suzanne's book had helped inspire my series, and I encouraged them to read it.

As we all know, the nation's economic situation had changed drastically between 2006 and 2011, and suddenly the message in *Through the Window of Life* felt much more realistic to readers. Demand for the book exploded, and we went through three printings in five months. Suddenly Suzanne was being asked again to speak, and she has willingly done so many times in the same humble way she always has.

Then in the summer of 2011 Suzanne told me she had a strong impression to focus on the nation's Founding Fathers. This came as a surprise to me, but then she reminded me she had met with them during her visit to the Spirit World, and they had pleaded with her to let everyone know of their concerns about the future of America.

Suzanne had devoted a chapter in her first book to her visit with the Founding Fathers, but that part of her experience had been overlooked when we focused on *Through the Window of Life*.

After talking with her, I read that chapter again. As I did so, it hit me like a thunderbolt that the time had come to emphasize their message. It hadn't resonated with me in 2005, but it certainly does now. We decided that a third book should be written, implementing portions of the first two books but emphasizing the important message the Founding Fathers had asked her to share with America.

Not so coincidentally, Suzanne had the opportunity to travel to the East Coast that autumn and visit many of the historical sites where the Founding Fathers shaped our country. She received many impressions about the threats to our liberty while she was there.

As you read this book, you'll recognize that the vital message the Founding Fathers gave Suzanne can assist us in not only restoring our nation, but in helping it achieve even greater glory.

SUZANNE'S INTRODUCTION

Throughout the ages, man has had a desire to be free. Thomas Jefferson stated in the Declaration of Independence that the pursuit of happiness is a God-given right, and that means we are entitled to have freedom.

Benjamin Franklin said, "Freedom is not a gift bestowed upon us by other men, but a right that belongs to us by the laws of God and nature." [1]

Thomas Jefferson believed the same thing, saying, "The God who gave us life, gave us liberty at the same time." [2]

God wants us to have liberty, and that desire is found in every living thing. When a wild animal is caught and caged, they look for any way to escape. The quest for liberty is never taken from them. Likewise, liberty is something we are born with. It is something we can keep in our hearts, whether we are oppressed by tyranny, or free. So we need to choose to have the spirit of liberty with us always.

Queen Esther inspires me because she was willing to risk her personal safety to save her people. Her story, found in the Old Testament book that bears her name, shows that God led her, step by step, to accomplish what was needed. God is the same now as He was then, and He will inspire and lead us just as He guided the people of old.

We don't realize that our liberties are taken from us gradually, a step at a time. It truly is like the frog who finds himself in a pot of warm water and blissfully floats as the heat slowly rises. He has no idea that he is being boiled until it is too late.

I know the United States of America was founded by God with the intention that we can have liberty and be happy. That's what God wants for us. I want you all to know that the Founding Fathers lived to give us a free land of liberty. They sacrificed the comforts of life, and some even gave up their fortunes for us.

I also know they loved Jesus Christ and knew Him personally. They wanted to serve Him in everything they did. This is how they lived their lives, for Christ. They loved Him more than life itself. They loved us enough to understand that even two centuries later we could still have a free country if we could hold onto the truths of Heaven.

I love the words of Ezekiel 33:1-9. I hope that those who love freedom will take them to heart and warn their neighbors that our liberty is in peril. It reads:

Again the word of the Lord came unto me, saying, Son of man, speak to the children of thy people, and say unto them, When I bring the sword upon a land, if the people of the land take a man of their coasts, and set him for their watchman:

If when he seeth the sword come upon the land, he blow the trumpet, and warn the people;

Then whosoever heareth the sound of the trumpet, and taketh not warning; if the sword come, and take him away, his blood shall be upon his own head.

He heard the sound of the trumpet, and took not warning; his blood shall be upon him. But he that taketh warning shall deliver his soul.

But if the watchman see the sword come, and blow not the trumpet, and the people be not warned; if the sword come, and take any person from among them, he is taken away in his iniquity; but his blood will I require at the watchman's hand.

So thou, O son of man, I have set thee a watchman unto the house of Israel; therefore thou shalt hear the word at my mouth, and warn them from me.

When I say unto the wicked, O wicked man, thou shalt surely die; if thou dost not speak to warn the wicked from his way, that wicked man shall die in his iniquity; but his blood will I require at thine hand.

Nevertheless, if thou warn the wicked of his way to turn from it; if he do not turn from his way, he shall die in his iniquity; but thou hast delivered thy soul.

I know the Lord wants us to follow that admonition. I want you all to know that I love the Lord. He is my best friend. He cries with me and he understands me perfectly. I know that He cares about me more than I could ever comprehend. I saw the prints of the nails in his hands and his feet. I remember his smile. It was perfect, beautiful and kind, filled with pure love. I know that He loves each one of us all the same.

I'm ever so grateful that He pushes me to do the things that make me better. I love Jesus with every fiber of my being. Without Him I am nothing. I feel his kindness and love. I have peace in my heart, knowing that I am protected and if I keep faith and hope in my life, I'll be as safe as the people were in the days of old. I am secure in the knowledge that there is peace wherever we are when we have Christ in our hearts.

As John 8:36 says, "If the Son therefore shall make you free, ye shall be free indeed."

My hope is that as you read these words, you'll find the spirit of liberty burning within you.

CHAPTER 1

Entering the Spirit World

The United States of America is a choice land. I have been blessed to live here throughout my life. Our freedom is fragile, though. During a near-death experience I met the Founding Fathers of the United States of America, and it was made clear to me that we must take action to preserve our liberty. I seek to share the Founders' message in greater detail, but first let me explain how I came to meet them.

In 1999, I suffered an ectopic pregnancy and died on a hospital surgery table. The embryo attached itself to the inside of my fallopian tube, and since there wasn't enough room there for a baby to grow, the tube ruptured and bled. I felt excruciating pain, and my body essentially turned into one big bruise.

I was rushed into surgery to save my life, but it was too late. My spirit left my body and floated up against the ceiling. It's a very odd sensation to gaze down at your own body, especially when it's lying on an operating table. I knew I was dead, but I also knew I couldn't stay that way. I enjoyed the relief from the pain, but I realized there were seven children at home who needed me.

My husband James, a trucker at the time, would never be able to care for all of our children and still provide a living for them. I worried that my children would have to be split up. I couldn't stand the thought of them being sent to different homes, maybe to never see each other again.

So I headed back toward my body without even glancing upward. My single goal was returning to my body, but before I could reach it, I was stopped suddenly by a hand encircling my arm.

Startled, I looked down at the hand. It was a man's hand, large and strong, with a puncture wound centered in the back. I knew I was staring at the hand of Jesus Christ. Filled with a sudden sense of awe, I looked up to see his blue eyes fixed on me in an expression of delight mixed with love.

Although my heart quickened in the presence of my Savior, I also felt a sense of panic. If Christ had come to get me personally, then it must really be my time to go! But I couldn't. My children needed me.

I tried to pull away to break Christ's hold on my arm and get back to my body before he could change my mind. Then with all the love in the world, Christ said, "There are people who want to see you."

I responded, "Then you'll have to bring them here, because I'm not going."

I didn't dare glance up at his face again for fear I wouldn't be able to stick to my resolve, but after a moment of silence, a hearty laugh rang out, startling me from my single-minded purpose. Christ was laughing! His laughter was like blending light with love, creating a sound of musical delight.

"I promise, you can come back," Christ said, and I quit struggling. When I looked up at Him again, I was surrounded by a love so complete that it was like nothing I'd ever felt anywhere on earth. Of course I would go with Him. I would follow Him anywhere.

We turned away from the operating room and faced a long flight of perfectly white stairs. There were no seams anywhere to be seen. The steps were faultless and made of a hard substance with a matte finish, like one solid piece of marble. The staircase was about twenty feet wide. We started climbing and went up several flights of stairs, which had occasional landings in between them. I climbed the stairs with ease. I was pleased to discover that my spirit body was slender and energetic.

I heard a heavenly choir of angels burst into glorious song. Every note was pitched to absolute perfection. I lifted my eyes toward the top of the stairs, trying to locate the source of the incredible voices that blended and harmonized and soared in a breathtaking melody.

Before I could locate the choir, I noticed gates at the top of the stairs. The closed gates were at least fifteen feet tall and made of gleaming gold bars twisted together into an intricate design. They were flawlessly crafted and beautiful to look upon. As we drew closer, I could make out the silhouette of a man's head in the exact center of each gate. It was a profile outlined in gold and set sideways, like an old-fashioned cameo. Each profile was surrounded by an oval of shining gold beads that gleamed with perfect symmetry and beauty. When we reached the gates, I recognized the profile as that of Jesus Christ.

The gates were hinged to heavy gold pillars on either side. Beyond the pillars stretched a golden fence with thin columns of gold curled and fashioned into intricate designs that were absolutely beautiful.

The gates swung inward, and a cheer went up from a throng of people who watched us enter. I was somewhat confused by all the commotion. My eyes focused on a familiar figure, and I stopped in my tracks.

"Grandma!" I called out before moving toward my Grandma Burton. I grabbed her in a long embrace. She looked younger than she had on earth, but the seventeen years that we'd been apart fell away, and it was as if she'd always been there for me.

"Hello, Suzie," she said, returning my affectionate squeeze. "It's so good to see you again."

I greeted many other relatives, including James'

Grandma Freeman, and I greeted her with as much joy as my own relatives. We all shared hugs and exclamations of delight at being reunited. Most of the family who greeted me had lived and died before I was born, yet even if I hadn't seen their photographs, I knew they were my family. The familial ties with them were not quite as strong as I had with those who had shared part of my earthly experience, but no matter how well I knew them, I was pleased to see and acknowledge them all.

We mingled in a beautiful garden, with perfectly smooth walkways that appeared to be made from the same seamless material as the stairway. The walks were lined with gorgeous flowers that were mesmerizing in their perfection. I was astonished that the flowers were actually swaying in perfect time with the music from the heavenly choir.

The grass was also perfect, with every single blade the same height, and each piece of grass was a brilliant green. People wearing white robes sat on the grass, talking to one another. The lawn was softer than the most luxurious carpet I'd ever felt. The deep azure blue sky was cloudless, and there was light everywhere, although there wasn't an obvious source.

At one point, Grandma Burton invited me to go with her to see her home, which was fashioned after the one I'd visited when she lived on earth in Afton, Wyoming. Her house was just the same as I remembered it, only everything was shiny and new. I suppose it looked just like it had in its prime in the 1930s.

Next, Grandpa Scholes showed me his apartment. I was surprised that it was small and sparsely furnished, not at all like the house he'd lived in on earth.

Before I could even ask him, Grandpa said, "This is my little bachelor pad." He winked at me, and I was sure he could read the confusion on my face. "I'm waiting for your grandma to get here so we can build our home in Heaven together."

Grandpa slid his arm around me. "Don't you worry about me for one minute, Suzie. I'm perfectly happy with this place. Besides, I'm hardly ever here anyway. I'm usually on assignment to help the grandkids in mortality."

I shared a warm hug with Grandpa, grateful to know that he would be assisting my children on earth.

Christ then introduced me to many people who had been prominent in earth's history, including the Founding Fathers of the United States of America, and it is their message that I want to share with you now.

CHAPTER 2

Meeting America's Founding Fathers and Hearing their Message to Our Generation

At this point during my journey in the Spirit World, Christ guided me up the steps of a splendid capitol building that had likely been built before the White House was even thought of. We entered a broad corridor with a wide-planked hardwood floor, polished to a high sheen.

Voices came from a room off to one side. When we pushed open the door, I saw George Washington standing behind a podium, addressing some of his peers from mortality, including many of the signers of the Declaration of Independence.

Washington looked in our direction as we entered the room, then smiled and came over to greet us. George Washington stands nearly 6' 4" and has broad shoulders. He's a quiet and gentle man, but he's firm in the things that matter. He's a deep thinker blessed with a gift to know just what to do in order to get the job done.

The affection between George Washington and Christ was quite evident, and it was reassuring to see that the first president of the United States is very close to the Lord.

After introducing me to Washington, Christ went around the room with me to meet Benjamin Franklin, Thomas Jefferson, John Adams, and other Founding Fathers of the United States of America. They seemed pleased to meet me, and Christ smiled at us while He stood at my side. His brotherly affection for all of them was apparent.

Soon, Abraham Lincoln strode into the room, leading a procession of other righteous presidents of the United States. Lincoln is kind and considerate, with his gentlemanly ways salted with just the right dash of wit and humor.

As I stood beside Jesus, I was shown in vision the earthly lives of many great people, such as the Founding Fathers, their mothers and wives, along with others who had filled important roles in our world's history.

I saw Thomas Jefferson writing out the Declaration of Independence, and George Washington leading troops into battle. Joan of Arc explained her life to me as I watched it happen. I saw the noble influence that the mothers of the Founding Fathers had held upon their lives, preparing them to become qualified, capable, God-fearing men. I also saw how the Founders' wives had played a key role as they supported and encouraged their patriot husbands.

One at a time, these great people came to stand beside the Savior and myself. I was given the privilege to observe key points from their lives, and I was taught how they had lived, what they had done, and why they had done it. It felt like I was watching a very realistic movie, but it was much more than that. It was as if I was literally a silent observer in the corner of the room where the actual events were happening.

As I watched these historic events, the leaders explained to me what they were thinking or feeling at that moment. This gave me a unique perspective. I saw each historical event unfold while being taught by the very person who lived it.

I hadn't realized how heavily some of their decisions had weighed upon them. They did remarkable things, but at a cost. The risks to themselves and their families were enormous and constantly present. I felt the weight of those risks and the significance of their choices as they decided to put the greater good before their own safety.

I watched the days of their youth, and I saw how they had been primed and prepared to serve God and their fellow men. I saw them accomplish great and wonderful deeds that helped pave the path of freedom for many future generations.

They shared with me their feelings of personal inadequacy, and the frustrations they faced as they tried to rally others to understand their cause. They told me how much God meant to them and how He had led them, helped them, and directed the beginnings of our nation.

They were excited to instruct me, and I enjoyed learning these wonderful things that only Heaven can teach. I understood so much about these great people, that I felt I truly knew them, and they became my friends.

THEIR MESSAGE TO US

I soon came to realize the Founding Fathers still have a deep interest in America many decades after their deaths. They care about us and our nation, and they are anxious that we preserve our liberties.

They let me know they are grieved at the state of our nation and are worried we are allowing our freedoms to slip away. They asked me to return to earth with the message that we should stand up for our rights and never allow them to be taken away. They are truly concerned that if we don't act quickly, America will become a forgotten nation.

The scripture found in Galatians 5:1 in the New Testament came to mind: "Stand fast therefore in the liberty wherewith Christ hath made us free, and be not entangled again with the yoke of bondage."

I knew the Founders were speaking from personal experience. They had lived at a time when the American Colonies were being exploited by a tyrannical British ruler. They made it clear that British troops were unwelcome in their cities, but they were sometimes forced to house British soldiers in their homes.

They were forbidden to trade unless it was with Britain, and this trade was heavily and unfairly taxed. The British Empire sought to direct all the Colonists' economic activities and was only concerned with the making profits for Britain. Parliament passed laws to regulate Colonial trade and denied the Colonists any say or representation in the lawmaking process. It was indeed "a yoke of bondage."

Mercy Warren was a patriot who wept over the way England treated the Colonies. She said, "America stands armed with resolution and virtue; but she still recoils at the idea of drawing the sword against the nation from whence she derived her origin. Yet Britain, like an unnatural parent, is ready to plunge her dagger into the bosom of her affectionate offspring."[1]

How keenly these early Americans must have felt the lack of freedom or choice and the strict control of their lives! No wonder they fought so hard to ensure that their descendants would not be under British rule. No wonder the Founding Fathers want us to ensure that the freedoms they secured for our country are never lost.

It was this sense of oppression that caused them to put their whole hearts and souls into the forming of this country by writing of the Declaration of Independence and establishing the Constitution. Every one of them either gave their life or would have willingly laid their life down in order to make sure that centuries later we would still have the rights and privileges that they wanted us to have and enjoy.

They are deeply saddened to see the rampant wickedness in our country today. They were righteous men during their time on earth who sought to do God's will. They raised their voices with intense passion to tell me how afraid they are for the future of the United States.

I was told, "If you take God out of our country, then God won't stay where He's not wanted. If Americans do not start living righteously and put God back into their lives, then the country will be taken from them."

With tears in their eyes, they told me how hard they'd worked to set up a place of freedom, and how deeply they believe in the United States of America. They said they would never have allowed references to God to be taken out of public places or schools or tolerated any kind of action that didn't allow calling upon God in prayer at any time. They urged me to let others know that we must stand up and not permit this to happen anymore. If we take God out of our schools, he will not stay where he is not invited.

I was told that if we do not put God back into all aspects of our life, whether it is in our own personal lives or as a nation, we will not be a free nation anymore, and the Heavens will weep. As Benjamin Franklin said, "Men will ultimately be governed by God or by tyrants."[2]

Patrick Henry rightfully observed, "It is when people forget God that tyrants forge their chains."[3]

I learned from an adamant Benjamin Franklin that the United States of America deserves whichever president is in office. If we are not living Godlike lives as a nation, we will not have a Godlike president.

Just before taking a prescribed dose of liquid mercury, which the physician stated would either kill him or cure him, Patrick Henry excused himself to pray for his family, his country, and his soul. The mercury proved fatal, and he left behind a will that mentioned to his family that the religion of Christ would make them rich indeed.

Our country's heritage was born of God, and also inspired and directed by God. We need to revive that heritage today.

Some of these righteous men who were early leaders of the United States, especially Thomas Jefferson, are incensed about the immoral stories that are circulating about them. There are many false stories of the Founding Fathers not acting in a goodly manner. These stories are just not true. How could these righteous men ever have received the inspiration they did, if those allegations were true?

Patrick Henry said, "Bad men cannot make good citizens. A vitiated state of morals, a corrupted public conscience are incompatible with freedom."[4] The lives of the Founding Fathers reflected this truth.

John Adams credited the powers of Heaven for placing him on earth at the same time with the other men who helped form the United States. The Lord's hand was indeed involved in bringing these great leaders together at such a crucial time in history.

It's no coincidence that many of the men who helped shape the United States were self-appointed teetotalers who also refrained from smoking in a day and age when no health problems or social taboos were associated with it. Patrick Henry even concocted a non-alcoholic barley drink that he offered for sale in his store as an effort to encourage men to abandon their whiskey.

We must remember that these were prayerful men who sought God's help. In 1787, Benjamin Franklin attended the Constitutional Convention in spite of the fact that he was sometimes in great pain and had to be carried to the meetings in a sedan chair. At one point, he humbly asked the assembly to consider prayer before debating issues important to the future of the country.

He reminded the assembly that in the war with Britain, their prayers had been answered.

Franklin said, "The longer I live, the more convincing proofs I see of this truth, that God governs in the affairs of men. I therefore beg leave to move that, henceforth, prayers imploring the assistance of Heaven and its blessing on our deliberations be held in this assembly every morning before we proceed to business."[5]

The men who signed the Declaration of Independence were, at one time or another, victims of manhunts, and were driven from their homes. Seventeen of them lost everything they owned, twelve had their homes burned to the ground, nine died as a result of the Revolutionary War, and five were brutally treated as prisoners of war. At least two had to suffer the pains of seeing their wives abused. Many of them tragically lost family members, and some even lost their entire families.

In 1777, John Adams wrote a letter to his wife, Abigail, saying, "Posterity! You will never know, how much it cost the present generation, to preserve your freedom! I hope you will make a good use of it. If you do not, I shall repent in Heaven, that I ever took half the pains to preserve it."[6]

I wish I could completely convey to you the passion the Founding Fathers have for America. Their depth of feeling is heartfelt and profound. This wasn't something they occasionally dabbled in, but rather something that had become part of their lives, and influenced their very makeup. They were ardent in explaining to me their intense and fervent desires for our country's future. They still believe in America, know of her greatness, and yearn for her future as a good parent longs for the best outcome for their child.

The Founding Fathers did what God asked of them. They were all God-fearing, honorable men and did what was appropriate in their day. None of them would have knowingly done anything against God's will. Their sacrifices and struggles for our freedom were immense. Now they ask us to keep their dreams alive in our hearts, to put God back into our country, and to take upon us the spirit of liberty. If we make this effort, their sacrifices become more meaningful and our future becomes brighter.

As Thomas Jefferson once said, "The price of freedom is eternal vigilance." [7]

CHAPTER 3

My Journey in the Founding Fathers' Footsteps

Not long after my first two books were published, I felt drawn to visit the historical sites where the Founding Fathers performed their God-given missions. After meeting these great men on the other side and seeing portions of their lives, this pilgrimage was something I *had* to do. I needed to place my feet where the Founding Fathers had walked, touch what they had touched, and feel the lingering spirit of their passion, as if I were in their presence again.

VALLEY FORGE

When I visited Valley Forge National Park, I could feel George Washington's presence as we toured the house he had stayed in that cold winter. I felt echoes of the other men, as I saw the locations where they had lived, worked, and sacrificed for our futures.

It was inspiring to see—nestled right within our modern world—the centuries-old places where they built our country and freedom began. Valley Forge was the winter encampment of the Continental Army under George Washington, and there is a feeling there that evokes the spirit of patriotism, independence, and collective sacrifice. The soldiers' suffering there demonstrated the willpower and fortitude and of those early Americans. These are traits I feel we still have today.

As I walked through the cabins where George's troops lived, I was surprised at how strong the spirit of freedom was there. I was also intrigued by the bread ovens, because I love to bake and can't imagine trying to create edible food with those fluctuating oven temperatures.

The troops suffered illness, cold, fatigue, hunger and homesickness. George did not expect them to stay and endure such conditions, but most of them did. Their desire to secure freedom was so strong that any physical discomfort they had to bear seemed small in comparison. They knew they were fighting to provide a better life for future generations.

I felt the prayers that George sent heavenward. He was completely aware his calling to lead the army was from God. Being in Valley Forge was truly like walking on sacred ground—a place made holy by those many prayers. I knew that God sent help to George and had guided him in his difficult task.

During this time, George was given a profound vision of our country's future which showed him what he was fighting for. This vision strengthened him during difficult times, and I've included an account of this vision in the Appendix.[1]

BOSTON

During my travels, I had only one day to visit the historic locations in Boston. I saw the Old North Church which was used to signal Paul Revere of the arriving British troops, who were also known as the "Regulars". One lantern was to be hung in the belfry arch of the steeple if the Regulars were seen coming by land, and two lanterns if they approached by sea.

As I walked in, I could feel the importance of the tall steeple on that church. At that day, it was the tallest structure in Boston, so it was just what was needed to hang the two lanterns that became the famous signal. They could only be hung for a few seconds so that the Regulars wouldn't see them.

Upon seeing the signal, Paul Revere rode to warn the townspeople that the Regulars were coming. They were able to send riders to even more towns, and they marshaled their militias as well. This was so effective that people living 25 miles away knew about the arrival of the British troops even as those troops were still unloading their boats in the harbor.

The time I spent at the actual places where these things happened helped solidify in my mind what I had seen while with the Founders in the Spirit World. It helped me see the complete picture of how God orchestrated everything that happened in America's history and prepared these great leaders to play their parts in freedom's cause.

My time was cut short, and I was unable to see much more of Boston, but I loved the spirit of the Revolution, and I felt drawn to go back. This persistent feeling wouldn't leave me for the next three years. It was as if the Founding Fathers and Patriots beckoned me to once again walk in their footsteps, and learn more about them.

So in the spring of 2011, I made the decision to return. I worked twelve-hour days and saved for three months to be able to take this trip back East with my friend Shari. I was also able to save up enough money to take my daughter, Coreena, along with us. Soon we were winging our way to the Colonial historic sites.

First we went to Lexington and Concord, where the first battles of the Revolutionary War were fought. Ralph Waldo Emerson described the first shot fired there by the Patriots as the "shot heard 'round the world,"[2] because of how it changed earth's history.

I felt honored to walk on the Village Green

where advancing British troops found 77 members of the Colonial Minute Men militia ready to defend Lexington.

I felt the emotion of the people who had lived in Lexington at the time of the Revolution. I knew they understood that they were preserving freedom for their great-grandchildren's grandchildren. They also knew they had to stop the British troops even at the cost of their own lives. Can you imagine fighting for something so profound that you would be willing to sacrifice everything? Their spirits were truly unbreakable!

I felt that same spirit of freedom at other locations in Lexington and Concord. I was able to see how the Patriots lived. As the tour guides explained the details of the people's daily lives, the Holy Spirit witnessed to me the truth of it all, and taught me even more.

At Paul Revere's home, I was impressed at how the women were able to cook over an open fire. I could envision the lives of the people, as they went about day to day. I heard the echoes of childbirth in a bedroom, and sensed the bustle of a meal being prepared at the hearth. I realized that as the floor was being swept, the fire made, and the bread kneaded, these women were thinking through their daily problems, worrying about family difficulties, and planning their futures, much as we do today.

I sensed the tender caress of a mother's hand on a child's head, and knew that genuine love had bound these people together, just like it does our families. These good people were just like us in that they worked, loved, and dreamed of a better future for their descendants.

I realized that only time and technology separated us. While a lame horse might throw a shoe in their day, a broken washer would complicate mine. We all work to maintain life, and figure out the problems that come our way to ensure a better future for those who come after us.

I put myself in their situations. If I was only allowed to buy from a single controlling source, and had to pay huge taxes on those purchases, I would feel the same as any housewife did back then! If our cities were occupied by foreign soldiers and we had no real say in our government, we certainly would make sacrifices to arrange a better future for our children!

They wanted freedom for their children, just as I want freedom for mine. They had families and joys just as we do, and yet they were willing to give up everything to obtain freedom for themselves, and their posterity. How strong their desire for liberty was! How great is my appreciation for what they did for us!

I went away with a perfect knowledge of the reasons why the Patriots fought against the British and desired to form their own nation. It touched my heart that these heroes, who so bravely fought for our freedoms, were family men. They were just average husbands and wives who knew it was a fight that needed to be fought. They did it without thought of glory or fame, and they did it for us. I will never forget the impression it left on me as I walked in the Founding Father's footsteps.

That yearning for freedom is what we must now rekindle in America before it is too late.

CHAPTER 4

Thomas Jefferson

In the following chapters I would like to share some important details I learned about several of the Founding Fathers, beginning with Thomas Jefferson. There was just something about him that impressed and moved me more than all of the other Founding Fathers. It was a true thrill to stand next to this great man as I was shown the events of his life.

Thomas' main mission in life had been to help secure our country's freedom. Even from a young age, the importance of freedom was so strong within him that it was like an obsession.

He once wrote, "I have sworn upon the altar of God eternal hostility against every form of tyranny over the mind of man."[1]

I could see the energy of his desire to serve the Lord in this capacity, and it was like an unmistakable force that surrounded him. Thomas felt insecure and unqualified for his part in our history, but he knew God would help him with the task. He knew his calling was important, and felt the Savior prompting and directing his work.

Thomas' writing ability was well known, and it was obvious to the other Patriots that he was the man who should draft the Declaration of Independence—the document that proclaimed the creation of an American people, claimed universal rights, and decreed America to be independent from the British Empire. This would become one of the most important documents ever written.

Thomas approached the task humbly and prayerfully, and he was blessed to be shown, as if in vision, how to word it. As I watched him write this document, I saw inspiration and ideas come to him as if they were little balls of light. As an idea came to him, he would mentally grasp onto it and write it down. Once that segment was written, another vital idea would be sent to him.

As Thomas was writing the Declaration of Independence, he became very aware that each word of the document was important. For this reason—despite all of the inspiration he was receiving—there were still many times when he would pause to search in books for needed information and ideas.

Partway through the task, Thomas was given a vision of how America would develop if he wrote a paragraph a certain way—and the effect it would have if he worded it differently. Through this process he was able to create a more powerful document. I even saw one moment when the Savior himself came and whispered in Thomas' ear as he wrote one crucial segment.

Thomas was also privileged to see in vision the country's existence from beginning to the end. This is something he kept private and sacred, but as he wrote the Declaration of Independence it was important for him to know what future generations of Americans would need.

In this vision he saw the nation being formed and the freedom that he would help create. He saw that citizens would be able to go to the church of their choice. He also saw the decisions of the nation's future leaders, both good and bad. It saddened him that some poor decisions would be made, but he also knew that freedom of choice was essential.

As he completed the Declaration of Independence, I saw him kneel in prayer asking God for approval of his work, and he was given assurance that the document was acceptable. Thomas wasn't aware of it at the time, of course, but as he said that prayer, I saw the Savior appear in the room. He put his hands on Thomas' head and said, "Good work, son." It brings me great comfort to know that Jesus Christ was deeply interested and involved in the creation of this document.

As we watched the concluding scenes of Thomas writing the document, he told me he truly felt the power of God surge through him as he worked on it. It was fascinating to hear his first-person perspective about these events. It was comparable to watching the "Director's Commentary" version of a favorite movie.

I was also shown Thomas taking this document to the other Founding Fathers and having them pick it apart, cut things out and change a few things. I could feel Thomas' emotions as they did this. He felt that it was exactly as God had wanted, and their reworking it like they did bothered him greatly.

However, he also understood that these men had knowledge and experiences that he didn't, so he humbled himself and made the changes. He also knew the document had to be approved by everyone since they were essentially signing their own death warrants by putting their signatures on it.

When the Declaration of Independence was finally signed, I felt the greatness of the moment—as well as the life-threatening consequences—for those who signed it. I saw angels comforting them by touching their shoulders or whispering in their ears, assuring them they had done a great thing that would stand the test of time.

Of course, Thomas also served our country as president. It wasn't easy for him to be in public office, but he did it for the greater good. He told me it was a "thankless job" and that he'd prayed to God, saying he didn't want to serve as president. In answer to this prayer, Thomas was given another vision and was shown who would take his place, and what would happen if he did not accept this calling.

After this vision, he better understood his role in history, and from then on Thomas accepted the role as U.S. president with a glad heart. He would spend his life serving God and his country, and he knew he would have time in the next life to pursue the hobbies and interests that he loved.

I was surprised to see that Thomas had struggled with public speaking. He was not eloquent. In fact, he was soft-spoken and a stutterer. He also had stage fright when speaking. There were many aspects of the presidential role that were difficult for him, yet he was still able to achieve great things.

Thomas brought about many admirable changes to the government. When he became president he stopped the ceremonial bowing that people did to greet the president, and offered his hand instead. He bought a round table so no one would be at the head. He also was the first president to have church held in the Capitol Building, and every Sunday there would be services in the Rotunda.

He felt that the presidential office was not to aggrandize him, but to serve the people. He wanted his great-great-grandchildren to live in a free nation.

One of my favorite quotes from Thomas is: "He who permits himself to tell a lie once, finds it much easier to do it a second and third time, till at length it becomes habitual; he tells lies without attending to it, and truths without the world's believing him. This falsehood of tongue leads to that of the heart, and in time depraves all its good dispositions."[2]

That statement shows us a glimpse into Thomas' great character. I learned from him that if we have a righteous desire and do our part, God will provide what is needed for us to complete our earthly tasks.

My hope is that I can learn and grow into what I was sent to earth to become. I want to *do* everything I can, not *have* everything I can. This is how Thomas felt as well.

CHAPTER 5

George Washington

As with every righteous man, George Washington had a burning desire to serve God. Great men know they were placed upon this earth to do God's will, and not to live only for themselves. They don't serve for the glory, or in hopes that their names will go down in history.

As I mentioned earlier, I could feel the Holy Spirit of God when I was in the house where George stayed during the winter at Valley Forge. This is where he had visions of what to do. Unfortunately, history hasn't always been recorded correctly, because some sacred moments have been left out of the accounts. As Thomas Jefferson said, "A morsel of genuine history is a thing so rare as to be always valuable."[1]

As I watched George grow to adulthood, I saw he resented the excessive control and harsh punishment the Colonists received from the British. He became frustrated with this unfair treatment and started making friends with those who were in the "know" about how unfairly England was exploiting the Colonies. This wasn't apparent to everyone at the time.

As George moved upward through the military ranks, he gained great respect among the Colonial troops. He loved and respected his men, and even though they were of low rank and did the grunt work, they felt he treated them well. He let them know every task they performed was vital, and everyone had an important place in their army.

George's reliance on God continued to grow during this phase of his life. He would kneel down in prayer before he would even start the day to ask for protection and guidance, and he always made sure to pray with the entire group of soldiers before leading his troops into battle. There were other prayers given in smaller groups, and individual prayers were encouraged.

There was so much protection from Heaven that the soldiers could feel it, and they knew that God was directing their fight for freedom. Many times a dense fog would roll in that protected the troops from the British soldiers.

Years before, George had taken part in the French and Indian War. The Indians, who said they knew the battle would be over if they killed the "white chief." So during each skirmish the Indians focused their attention on killing George. They succeeded in wounding him, but he couldn't be killed.

The Indians realized George was the "Great White Prophet" who their tribal leaders had prophesied would someday take over their nation. This leader would be great in battle and ride a white horse, and although their best warriors would shoot their arrows straight and true, they would not be able to hit him.

As I stood with George as we watched his life unfold, he explained to me that during this battle he knew the Indian warriors were targeting him with their arrows. However, the Spirit of God told him to have peace and not be afraid. He knew he would be protected from the deadly arrows, and though he might be wounded it would not be enough to keep him from leading his men to victory.

I could see the actual shield of safety that the Heavens placed over him, like a force field. I could also see protecting angels directing the arrows or bullets away from him.

God sustained him in miraculous ways over the years. George acknowledged more than sixty desperate moments during the struggle for independence when he would have suffered disaster if the hand of God hadn't intervened.

It was during the challenging winter of 1777 in Valley Forge that George knelt down in humble prayer and was given a grand vision of the birth, progress, and destiny of the United States. This vision helped strengthen his resolve in the face of seemingly imminent defeat.[3] (See the appendix for the complete account of this vision.)

When the Revolutionary War was finally won, the Colonies needed a leader to guide the new nation. Many people wanted George to be their king, but he declined, knowing the danger it could bring upon the nation in future years. The Colonies had just freed themselves from the clutches of a dominating king, and George didn't wish for another monarchy to be imposed upon them.

George had replied, "Let me conjure for you, then, if you have any regard for your Country, concern for yourself or your posterity, or respect for me, to banish these thoughts from your mind and never communicate, as from yourself or anyone else, a sentiment of the like nature."[2]

Instead, George said he would serve as their president. He knew God was directing the formation of this new nation, and he was pleased that this new form of government would help ensure that no individual would have absolute ruling power. The power would be spread throughout the three branches of government to help maintain freedom for all citizens and reduce the chance of a dictator rising up to mislead the people.

George was a man called by God to do incredible things with far-reaching effects that still bless our lives today. I'm so very glad that I got to know him.

CHAPTER 6

James Madison

As my visit in the Spirit World continued, James Madison joined me. A vision soon opened up of young James in his home, where his mother was teaching him. He was intelligent and a quick thinker, and she encouraged him to seek out knowledge about the world around him. I could see an actual light become part of him as his mother taught him with kindness and love.

When I add that experience to the information I've read about him, it gives me a more comprehensive picture of this man, and indeed of all men that God calls to perform great tasks in behalf of mankind. They have a personal strength, a fire within, and a knowledge that they are nothing without God's help.

I found it interesting that most of the time these men had prepared for their callings by studying certain topics as children, not knowing why they have such a voracious appetite for learning these subjects. This acquired knowledge becomes a well that they draw upon as adults to perform extraordinary deeds that help many people.

James was called the Father of the U.S. Constitution because he had the sacred task of writing it. I know that he studied and prepared as a young man so he would be ready and qualified when the time came for it to be written. It was not by luck nor by accident that he happened to be at the right place and at the right time in history.

As a youth he had studied ancient and modern governments. Like Thomas Jefferson, he was a gifted writer, but he was also known for his speaking ability. John Marshall, who served as Chief Justice of the United States Supreme Court, said, "Mr. Madison was the most eloquent man I ever heard."[1]

The Constitution was so important to James that he often prayed for assistance from above, asking that God would be with him as he wrote. He prayed that the pen he was holding would be an instrument in God's hands. He sensed the Constitution was going to be used for many generations, and that other countries would model their own constitutions after it.

When James was young, his parents could see there was a problem with the way the British were controlling and exploiting the Colonies. They had a deep faith in God, and that liberty came from God. They knew that religion was very important, and that there were many different beliefs, but they firmly believed that it was paramount that they should be allowed the right to choose their own religion and worship as they pleased. This is the agency that God wanted for this free country. Their opinions helped shape James' own way of thinking.

Little is known about the families of the Founding Fathers, but I was shown how their mothers taught them and prepared them for their future callings. These mothers taught their sons the importance of love, kindness, and mercy. My heart grieves for the family situations many children find themselves in today.

I learned that most of the Founding Fathers were blessed to have faithful fathers who taught them the importance of respect, honor, and humility. However, it was shown to me that it truly takes a village to raise a child. God made sure there were many good people in the lives of these young men who helped them stay on the right course and help them achieve what they were called to do.

Despite strong training in his youth, James still had to prove himself worthy for such a calling. He had to study and listen to the promptings of the Holy Spirit to learn what he could about our personal liberties. What a wonderful thing it is to know there were men who loved God enough to listen to the Holy Spirit's whisperings!

As James worked on the Constitution, he felt

Heaven was looking down on him while he was writing it. He was right. It was like the roof opened up, and many angels watched this important event happen.

I saw great kings and ancient prophets prompt him as he wrote it. I saw them literally whisper in his ear. The prophet Moses seemed to be the key person who assisted him, but many others were there as well. The room was often full of righteous spirits—a true "standing room only" event!

James fully understood the Constitution was the foundation our government would stand upon. He knew that it had to be worded precisely so it would not be misunderstood. He hoped the Constitution would be used for many hundreds of years.

James once said, "A popular government without popular information or the means of acquiring it is but a prologue to a farce or a tragedy, or perhaps both. Knowledge will forever govern ignorance: And a people who mean to be their own Governors, must arm themselves with the power which knowledge gives."[2]

James Madison certainly armed himself with knowledge, and had the spiritual stature of a giant.

From my experience with James I learned that if we make a valiant effort to seek out knowledge and learn our duty, then the heavens will open up and help us fulfill our purpose in life. What a lesson for us in our lives today! What an example he is!

CHAPTER 7

Benjamin Franklin

Benjamin Franklin was one of the most passionate of the Founding Fathers that I met. He showed me his strong zeal for America.

As with the other Founding Fathers, I watched Benjamin Franklin's life while he and the Savior stood beside me. I instantly sensed the importance of the role he played in our history.

One aspect I really enjoyed was seeing Benjamin as a young man. We tend to picture him as an old man, but in his youth he was energetic and witty. I realized that same personality had continued on in the Spirit World when he joked with me and called me his "sidekick" as we watched scenes from his life,

As we know from history, Benjamin had also been blessed with great wisdom and intelligence. He had a brilliant mind that God could mold into a man that could be used for righteous purposes. I saw that during his life Benjamin somehow had an open line with God—it was like a steady light pointing toward heaven. He suffered through his share of frustrations and failures, though, which helped keep him humble.

He loved to invent things, which indirectly led to his passion about freedom. He knew that without liberty his ability as an inventor would be restricted. He told me, "I wouldn't have been able to invent things if I was a slave."

I saw how angels inspired him to create inventions that were frontrunners to future inventions, such as his experiments with electricity that paved the way for our modern way of life. Benjamin was too busy pondering and doing experiments to realize he had angels around him, but they were there nonetheless.

I saw the angels send light from heaven to him, which literally appeared like a light switch was turning on in his head. He worked feverishly when these ideas came, and he learned to quickly write them down before they left him. Often he worked hard on one invention so he could move on to the next one.

Each invention usually led to another idea. It was like the light from heaven would not turn off. The Lord truly used him to benefit mankind in many ways.

Despite his genius as an inventor, Benjamin's most important calling was to help form a new nation. As he began dealing with the British government officials, he realized how corrupt the British Parliament truly was. In 1764 the Currency Act was imposed upon the

Colonies. In response, Benjamin sailed overseas to speak to Parliament in hopes of putting a stop to the continual "taxation without representation" that was occurring.

When Benjamin arrived in England he saw great poverty. Beggars were in the streets. As he spoke to Parliament, he began to understand why. He sensed these men only cared about wealth and power.

I could see the light of God that was with Ben as he spoke. He made a strong impression on those leaders, but he knew that in the long run the Colonies would need to separate from England.

As I watched these scenes with Benjamin, I could read the evil thoughts of those men and saw evil spirits rejoicing when the leaders would pass a law to enslave the Colonies. These demons would laugh as they would whisper in the ear of British leader and watch him repeat their words. These demons gained perverse pleasure in knowing they were causing great trials for everyone. They knew they were about to start a war and they reveled in the fact that they are causing great pain in both sides of it. It helped me remember that there is opposition in all things, and we must do all we can to stay on the Lord's side and not be influenced by the adversary's minions. .

When Ben came back to the Colonies, he knew without a shadow of a doubt that there was no other option than to separate from their mother country

England. This saddened him greatly, and he sent a troubled prayer toward heaven, knowing that good men on both sides would lose their lives because of the selfish British leaders. But he knew without question that heaven was on the Colonies' side.

As we watched this scene, Benjamin pointed out that a key part of his earthly mission was to discover Parliament's true intentions. Otherwise, it might have been many more years before the Colonists would have dared take the necessary steps to form their own country.

Like the other Founding Fathers, Benjamin knew that by signing the Declaration of Independence he was risking his life. When he signed that document at age 81, he wept with emotion.

I had a pure understanding that Benjamin Franklin really loved God, and he knew that without God in our country, there could not be liberty. On this subject he once said, "I have lived, Sir, a long time, and the longer I live, the more convincing proofs I see of this truth— that God Governs the affairs of men. And if a sparrow cannot fall to the ground without His notice, is it probable that an empire can rise without His aid?"[1]

During this wonderful visit with Benjamin, I realized that events in our lives don't happen by accident. I know when we do our part, God is bound to do His part as well. He wants us to do good, productive things in our lives. The angels in heaven rejoice when we do, but they also weep when we don't. I know making the right choices will enable us to help others, even if it is just to spread a little good cheer. There is always something each of us can do.

I know that when we die and meet the Lord, He will ask how we treated our fellow man. That is what God will ask of us—not what kind of car we drove or how much money we had in the bank.

Benjamin is a powerful example of focusing on those around us, because as an inventor he could've concentrated solely on his various projects and become wealthy without any regard for the welfare of his neighbors. But in the end, he sacrificed everything for his fellow countrymen and his God. Now, after getting acquainted with him, I know he wouldn't have had it any other way.

CHAPTER 8

Joan of Arc

I have been so inspired by Joan of Arc. Although she lived in the early 1400s, long before the Founding Fathers were born, she helped reignite the flames of liberty in Western civilization. So while I was surprised at first that she was part of the group I visited with in Heaven, it made perfect sense.

Joan was poor peasant girl who had a great calling in life. She was shown visions and trained by angels in order to save France. As she learned more about her mission, she didn't want to go to battle. She actually pleaded to get out of the frightening future that the angels were preparing for, saying many times that she just wanted to stay home with her mother.

Then she was taken up in vision once again and shown two scenarios: what would happen if she chose to avoid her mission, and what would occur if she fulfilled it. She was shown that if she rejected her calling that

France would be taken over by England, and her people would be wrongfully imprisoned as they lived under English law. However, if she accepted it, she could help defeat England and make France free. Thankfully she followed God's will and rallied France's demoralized troops. She changed the course of history—and our future as well.

She needed to accomplish what she did so that America could be free. Does that sound surprising? I'll explain: France helped finance the American Revolution. France was looking for a way to undermine England and thought that helping the American Colonies would do just that. The French sent funds, weapons, uniforms, and supplies to the Colonies, along with troops and naval forces.

By doing so, they quite possibly tipped the outcome of the war in America's favor. They couldn't have done this if they'd been conquered by England during Joan's time.

I saw Joan's life in the same way I saw the Founding Fathers' lives, watching key parts of her life while she stood at my side. I didn't see her gather eggs or milk the cow, but I saw and felt the thoughts and feelings she had as the angels were explaining to her what her mission would be. She was young, unmarried, and without any ties in life at all. Perhaps she had to be a pure maiden to hear those voices and see visions.

I sensed her feelings of inadequacy and fear as

she questioned the angel Michael, who showed her the battles she would fight. However, I also saw the power and the peace that was given to her by the angels administering to her. Sometimes the angels had to speak convincingly to get her to do what God had asked of her, but she eventually did so.

I saw Michael give her strength in the form of a ball of light that was placed within her chest. I could see a change come over her after receiving this power from heaven. Her love for God grew and she gained an inner peace that the outcome of her life would be the way God intended it to happen.

By the time her mission began, she had perfect faith and such love for The Master that she was willing to give her life for the truth. It didn't matter to her if she died. It only mattered that she would please the Lord.

Joan was angry at the apathy the French people felt toward the English invaders. They were content to be conquered without a fight. The angels taught Joan that this indifference was wrong. France had to be free!

The French troops were also demoralized with many losses in battle, so Joan rallied them to fight for their freedom. She told them, "In God's name, we must fight them! If they were hanging by the clouds we should get them; for God sends us to chastise them!"[1]

As Joan and the Savior stood beside me, she told me of her failings and how unqualified she had felt. She explained how it was to be a young girl in her day, when men felt women were only supposed to cook, clean, weave, and give them sons—not lead grown men into battle. The challenge was greater than she thought possible, but she knew with God's help she could—and must—do it.

Joan was given the gift of discernment. She used this gift often in her calling. For example, she picked out the true King of France, who was hiding among his men dressed in plain clothing. They tried to trick her, but she wasn't able to be deceived.

She was also given physical strength equal to that of many men, through the power of God. The strongest warrior became tired before she did. The Spirit of God was so strong in her that she could fight for days, and she was able to defeat any man in battle.

With every new battle she was given guidance by the Lord through a vision of what she needed to do in order to defeat the enemy. Then sometimes after the vision ended, it was repeated so she could remember it with certainty.

I watched Joan being led to discover an old sword that had been concealed in a castle. This sword had been hidden for a long time, just for her use. It was sacred, and had been blessed by a man of God. The sword's purpose was to help preserve freedom and righteousness, and never to be used for tyranny or wicked designs. The sword was large and made for a strong man with broad shoulders who could wield it during battle, not for a young maiden. God blessed her with strength to be able to handle this large sword for his purposes. In addition, Joan was also given sword-fighting skills as if she'd had years of experience. As we watched a battle scene, Joan told me she just had to hold the sword and it would do what was needed.

She could not ride a horse before her mission began, but her heavenly teachers showed her how to ride one because it was necessary for her mission. Then she simply mounted the horse and rode off, as if she had been riding for years.

Joan was so spiritually gifted that she could see and feel her heavenly help. I saw the assistance she received, and when she asked, it came to her. Even when she escaped from prison she was helped. She jumped out a high tower window into a dry moat and was not harmed.

The soldiers Joan dealt with were crass, but she wouldn't allow any foul language in the army. She once heard a merchant cursing God, and declared, "Ah, friend, dare you thus foreswear our Lord and Master? In God's name, you will recant before I leave here!"[2]

The French people needed to display humility before they could become free, and the soldiers gained it under Joan's leadership. It took humility for those men to be led by a young maiden, and God helped them as they followed her humble example. She didn't put herself above other people.

For example, women would bring her objects to touch, thinking Joan's touch would make the objects into powerful, sacred relics. Joan merely laughed and said, "Touch them yourselves. They will be quite as good with your touch as mine!"[3]

As I watched her life, I sympathized with how lonely she was. In reality, the angels were her only friends. She longingly spoke of hopefully one day rejoining her family and tending their sheep when her sacred task was completed. The people around her didn't understand her calling, and she didn't share details with others about the sacred mission she'd been entrusted with.

Despite her humility, Joan was bold when needed. She had scribes send out letters to the English, warning them of what would happen to them if they would not listen to her. In one she said, "You, men of England, who have no right to this Kingdom of France, the King of Heaven orders and notifies you through me, Joan the Maiden, to leave your fortresses and go back to your own country; or I will produce a clash of arms to be eternally remembered. And this is the third and last time I have written to you; I shall not write anything further!"[4]

In two short years she helped save the nation of France. Joan was like Queen Esther, who saved her Jewish people from captivity and persecution in Persia. Queen Esther interceded with the king in behalf of her people at the risk of her own life. Like Joan, Queen Esther completed a remarkable, sacred task.

When Joan was captured and tried, she gave a warning to her interrogators by saying: "You say that you are my judge; take good heed of what you do, because, in truth I am sent by God, and you put yourself in great peril."[5]

Joan was condemned to be burned to death. Her last request was for a cross. As she was being burned, she asked that the crucifix be held up in front of her so she could gaze upon it, saying, "Hold the cross high, that I may see it through the flames."[6]

As her life ebbed away, her last words were, "Jesus, Jesus, Jesus!"[7]

Joan's life truly was pure and Christlike to the end. Twenty-five years after her death, Pope Callixtus III pronounced her innocent and a martyr. In 1920 she was canonized, although I know she wouldn't want the worldly glory that came from it.

Without Joan's valiant efforts, the world would be a different place. No wonder she is called "the Mother of Freedom" and her story has been told through the centuries. She was a simple peasant girl, young and terrified, but full of the spirit of liberty. Her example shows us that even if we think we are unqualified, we can accomplish whatever God asks of us.

Joan's life and example touched me deeply. She truly earned her spot as a forerunner to our freedoms.

CHAPTER 9

The Ladies of Liberty

When we think of the heroes of the American Revolution we must include the mothers and wives of those great men. Their roles were every bit as important in the fight for freedom.

They firmly believed in the cause of liberty and publicly declared, "Let it be known unto Britain, even American daughters are politicians and patriots, and will aid the good work with their female efforts."[1]

I call them the Ladies of Liberty because they were outright and unsung heroes who made bold protests at the risk of their lives, yet they also worked quietly behind the scenes. They kept the fires and farms going while loving, supporting, and serving their husbands and sons. They often knew what was going on in the community better than the men did, and they used this information to further the cause for freedom.

It is said that the nature of a woman's heart is to fight for her offspring. No matter how afraid she is, she will fight like a mama grizzly bear to protect her cubs. Men often fight for land, money, or control, but a woman defends her children, and grandchildren, even if she has to fight to her death to do so. This willingness to sacrifice themselves for their posterity gives women the power to be ferociously effective in any fight.

One of those early female patriots, Mercy Warren, a good friend of Abigail Adams, wrote: "May nothing ever check that glorious spirit of freedom which inspires the patriot in the cabinet, and the hero in the field, with courage to maintain their righteous cause, and to endeavor to transmit the claim to posterity, even if they must seal the rich conveyance to their children with their own blood."[2]

One example took place at the time of the Boston Tea Party. While the men hid in Indian costumes as they dumped British tea into the harbor, more than fifty women met at Elizabeth King's home and signed a pledge vowing to boycott the buying of English dresses. That's bravery!

They risked not only their lives, but since many of their husbands were merchants who traded with England, they risked their husband's livelihoods as well. They boldly declared to the enemy: "We, the aforesaid Ladyes, will not promote ye wear of any manufacturer from England until such a time that all acts which tend to enslave our native country shall be repealed."[3]

The English leaders thought these women weren't

able to make their own fabric and clothing and had forbidden the Colonists to trade with anyone else. They supposed the only source of dresses was from England. Little did they know that Colonist women could—and did—make their own materials and dresses.

This brave stance is only one of many courageous acts of these Ladies of Liberty, and makes me think of Dolley Madison.

Dolley became a widow at a young age after her husband and infant son died of yellow fever. Then she met and married James Madison, who became the vice-president to Thomas Jefferson.

Thomas was a widower and therefore had no one to help him host official parties or to welcome foreign diplomats when he began his presidency. Dolley graciously took over that duty, adding a woman's touch. She then continued in that role when her husband served as the nation's fourth president. Dolley was kind, caring, and gave the White House guests a wonderful welcome. Her bubbly personality was an asset and helped smooth over political tensions among the guests. She became the icon of First Ladies.

Dolley had the spirit of freedom, and loved her country as much as her husband did. She knew that women had an important role in the making of America. The men would absolutely not be able to do it alone.

The women used their influence for good, by

teaching young boys and girls how to be responsible citizens. I truly believe the saying, "The hand that rocks the cradle, rules the world."[4]

Along those lines, I tell my son that "a man who treats his wife like a princess was raised by a queen."[5] A good woman's influence is felt for generations.

Dolley also knew the importance of preserving American history even while the country was still young. Dolley often worried about these things more than her own personal belongings.

For example, during the War of 1812 Dolley got word that the British were on their way to occupy Washington D.C. The White House staff nervously scanned the horizon with telescopes for signs of the invaders. Dolley knew the British would loot and destroy everything they could find. So she quickly had the White House staff gather up important documents, some silver, and the painting of George Washington, which was a symbol of the new republic.

The full-length painting was screwed to the wall, but she had them break the frame and roll up the canvas. She wrote to her sister: "It is done . . . the precious portrait placed in the hands of gentlemen for safekeeping. I am accordingly ready; I have pressed as many Cabinet papers into trunks as to fill one carriage; our private property must be sacrificed, as it is impossible to procure wagons for its transportation."[6]

Staff members who were directing their escape

were frustrated at Dolley for her delay, but she felt it was important to preserve the symbolic painting.

When the British invaded Washington, D.C. they took almost everything the Madisons owned. When the Madisons returned to the White House three days later, they found it burned to the ground. Dolley's courage and sacrifice preserved those historic items for us at the cost of her personal belongings.

Martha Washington is another Lady of Liberty that comes to mind. She was often alone during the Revolutionary War while her husband George as commanding the troops. She knew that at any time she could receive a message that he had been killed.

This was a worry shared by all women whose sons and husbands were fighting for liberty. Freedom is not free—there is a heavy, heart-wrenching, painful price. As a wife, and a mother of seven sons, I could hardly bear losing even one of them. I think of the sleepless nights those ladies must have endured, crying out to God for the protection of their loved ones. Those wonderful ladies made it through those tough times with their heads held high.

Martha once wrote, "I am determined to be cheerful and happy in whatever situation I may find myself. For I have learned that the greater part of our misery or unhappiness is determined not by our circumstance but by our disposition."[7]

While in the Spirit World, I was privileged to meet

many of these Ladies of Liberty. They all came into a great room that looked as if it might have been in the White House. They were dressed in the clothing of their day, complete with frills and hoops. Their hair had lovely curls, and some wore small hats. They were beautiful beyond description, and I felt I was in a room filled with queens. These women were majestic!

Their nobility and strength was apparent. I have never before seen such poise, beauty, or grace. Their countenances glowed with their love of God, and I could sense their great intelligence. I could feel their strength, and their fervent desire of freedom for their descendants. I can feel it just as strong now as when I was on the other side. I will never forget it.

Their message to me was that they were just as much patriots as their sons and husbands were. I could feel the influence that they'd had on their sons. They had known that they were raising great men to do great things. The mother of George Washington particularly impressed me. She'd known the importance of raising strong sons.

This crucial role, which they filled so well, produced men of strength and righteousness that God could later call upon to fill important roles in the founding of our country. We must do the same.

These faithful women emphasized to me that today's mothers need to teach their children to know and love God, and to pray to Him often. They must teach the scriptures in their homes and share the importance of following the Savior.

We can change the world just by teaching children to be kind, thoughtful, and to love one another. I hope we realize the importance of the work we do as mothers. Teaching our youth to love God, and each other can do more good than we will ever know. What an effect a woman can have on the world! The establishment of America would have been much more difficult without the Ladies of Liberty!

CHAPTER 10

Why Thomas Jefferson and John Adams Both Died on July 4, 1826

As I've studied history I have been fascinated in the fact that Thomas Jefferson and John Adams both died on July 4, 1826, the fiftieth anniversary of the signing of the Declaration of Independence. This was not a mere coincidence. This was to seal up the truth of their beliefs, like martyrs had done in the past.

They had lived their lives for liberty, and they did it for us. So when they died on the Fourth of July, it was to show the world that the fight for freedom was real and important. Their deaths on this special date emphasized one of the most important documents ever signed in the history of mankind.

When the document was signed by 56 men on July 4, 1776, they sensed that millions would flock to this nation for the freedom to work as they wished, worship

God as they chose, and have the right to live their lives as they wanted to. They knew that their years of toil would result in a glorious country that would last for many generations. Later, other nations would copy their basic pattern of government to improve their own countries.

Thomas Jefferson died at his home in Virginia at age 83. He died from a combination of pneumonia, infections, and severe diarrhea.

John Adams died at age 91 in Massachusetts. He succumbed to heart failure after giving a final toast to "independence forever."

Thomas and John were both very ill and unaware of the other's condition. Thomas asked if it was the Fourth of July, and he was told that it was. A few hours later he slipped into a coma and then died.

Thomas' last words were, "Is it the Fourth? I resign my spirit to God, my daughter and my country." [1]

John died a few hours later. Just before he died he said, "Thomas Jefferson lives."[2]

Is it possible he saw his old friend come to escort and welcome him to the other side? I believe so.

It is also interesting to note that five years later, on the same date, James Monroe died at age 72 in New York City of tuberculosis and heart failure.

I believe that the Fourth of July was so very important to these men that their deaths on that day testified of their unshaken belief in America.

CHAPTER 11

My Vision of America's Future

Toward the end of my visit with America's founders, I asked Jesus, "What is America's future?" I wasn't certain I really wanted to know. You'd think I would've learned not to ask questions, because sometimes I get answers that are difficult to accept.

I had learned that Jesus didn't force difficult information on me. The desire for such knowledge had to come from within my heart, and after I asked the question, he would provide the answer.

The Savior explained to me that there are multiple choices and possible outcomes in America's future. There could even be a combination of these results, but there were three scenarios that were shown to me.

I was taught that we never truly know the exact future because our individual and collective choices change the outcome. If we make certain choices, one thing could happen and if we made another choice, a different event could occur. I was told that nothing is set in stone, other than the Savior will come again at the Second Coming in all of His glory.

So we can change what will happen with our choices, and that means we are more powerful than we think we are. We have the power to shape the course of the future.

When Jesus showed me the vision, He looked upon me with great love and kindness. It made me wish that everyone on earth could understand the greatness of His love. I knew He didn't want his children to suffer more than what was needed for our growth and understanding. Without that growth and understanding, we would not progress in our spiritual development or cry to Him in prayer. I could feel his love and hope for those who would hear the messages of warning that the Heavens were sending to the earth.

I know Christ showed me this vision so we could understand that we have the power to choose, even though "the powers that be" seem to make the choices for us. I also saw that He will prepare places of safety for the righteous to escape the challenging times that will soon be upon us. These are places where we will have love and joy while awaiting the Coming of the Lord.

I was shown a few different ways in which the future might develop according to the decisions we will make. Even these results could vary, and I did not see everything. I only know what my understanding of the future was at the time of this vision.

There are things I don't understand and therefore I might not have noted every possible angle. I also see things through the optimism of rose-colored glasses, and I have a hard time focusing on the bad and ugly, so I tend not to report those aspects. I can look at these difficult things when I have to, because I know that through faith, anything is possible. We grow through adversity and I have certainly grown from the things the Lord has taught me, even the difficult and frightening things.

When I was shown the different ways America could fall, I learned that some people would not have to endure the coming difficulties exactly the same way as the unprepared will. Although they might not have the type of home or food they were used to, they did have a sense of peace that could only come from above. They had a perfect knowledge that there would be something great coming, and that it would be necessary for our learning and development.

If there is hope, there is peace. I know this, and I saw it happen over and over in the vision that Jesus gave me. I saw angels of peace coming to help those who had faith and hope even in the most difficult. When there was hope, there was help.

I could see that those with hope had the spirit of liberty shining in their hearts. It was a gift from the Heavens that could never be taken from them.

I knew that America had reached this point of vulnerability through a series of decisions, particularly after the beginning of the 21st Century. The United States had weathered other challenging times, such as the Great Depression in the 1930s, the Watergate crisis in the 1970s, and the Iran-Contra scandal in the 1980s.

However, it was the attacks that occurred on September 11, 2001 that launched America on its current course. That tragedy sparked the creation of the Patriot Act, which has led to greater government involvement and scrutiny of the everyday lives of Americans. The attacks also sparked the reorganization of many U.S. government agencies, and in 2003 the United States Department of Homeland Security was formed with the goal of reducing terrorism within the United States. These decisions by our national leaders were well-intentioned, but they have led to situations that could potentially limit or even take away our liberty.

Both the George W. Bush and Barack Obama presidential administrations greatly expanded the government's reach through executive orders and other mandates that have led us to our current situation. President Obama's election in 2012 to a second term in office means the same tactics will likely continue.

As I was shown the events of our country's future, I understood that it is important to know how to listen to the Spirit of the Lord, and to make sure that we do as He directs. This will help us to know what to do when difficult situations arise. There is always a way out of difficulties for those who know how to follow the Spirit of God.

As you read this, please keep in mind that these things do not have to happen in the exact way that I saw them in vision. These are only *possibilities* based upon our changeable decisions. So with that being said, I will tell you what I learned while I was in the presence of the Lord.

TYRANNY

It has been said, "A caged canary is secure; but it is not free. It is easier for free men to resist terrorism from afar than tyranny from within." [1]

The first scenario I was shown was one of total tyranny in which our rights as U.S. citizens were completely taken away by our own government. I was shown that it happened gradually in a way that initially sounded good, as if they were doing us a favor, while their actions were really designed to remove our freedoms. People didn't realize it until it was too late.

It occurred to me that it was like plucking a wing feather, once a day, from a beautiful bird. The bird can still fly until too many wing feathers are plucked, then suddenly the bird has lost the power of flight.

The government will further mislead the citizens by saying that we would all be better off if we helped each other by merely pooling our resources together.

As I watched this possible outcome unfold, I saw a few good people who helped one another, but more often I saw people not wanting to help a stranger. These people were selfish, and this selfishness made it easy for the government leaders to take over and give power to the rich and the thoughtless.

Those seeking power became wealthy, and they took control over the rights of the common people. This was a great surprise to those who wanted to get government help. They were promised many things, but the flamboyant person serving as president took control and did what he wanted to serve himself, all the while stealing from the common man. All he cared for was becoming a man of power.

Children were taught in school to get a job, and to never start their own businesses. The government purposefully made it difficult to own a small business. There was greed, control, and corruption, and while big industries prospered, the people were pushed deeper into poverty. It was explained to me that the government is a reflection of the people. If the people are wicked and corrupt, their government will be also.

I saw brightness around some people. They still had hope, even during the difficult times. They trusted in God and made the choice to be happy, while they waited for God to deliver them.

I hope that this wonderful country can be saved. I look at the inspirational examples of our Founding Fathers, and people like Joan of Arc. They changed the course of history through the spirit of liberty burning strong in their hearts. I am convinced that if we take the spirit of liberty into our hearts, we will have freedom in any situation. Margaret Mead once said, "A small group of thoughtful people could change the world. Indeed, it's the only thing that ever has."[2]

Then the vision shifted and I saw another future possibility being portrayed.

PROMISED HELP FROM THE GOVERNMENT NOT FORTHCOMING

In this scenario, I was shown that people wanted to have as much help as possible from the government with food, housing, and health care. So they elected a president they thought would do just that—help the people. But when he became president he didn't do what he had promised, and he didn't care about the common person. All he wanted was power, and the decisions he made caused the people to suffer greatly.

Food got even more expensive, and wages did not follow inflation. The food costs were so high that it wasn't long before the children went hungry. Many citizens would go to bed starving each night.

It was a great surprise to the people how quickly this happened.

Health care was practically unavailable. If a child broke his arm there was no way to get the help he needed. People had to sign up on a long waiting list for medical treatment, and it didn't matter how urgent the injury was, they still had to wait their turn. A broken arm was not considered an emergency.

Prescription medications were hard to get, and strong pain medications were illegal. The government controlled these things, and the people who needed them the most could not get them. The black market was big, and for a high price, they sold things that are easily bought in stores today.

Most women today have their babies in the hospital, but not in this scenario. Birthing was not considered a medical emergency, and doctors were not allowed to conduct births in the hospitals.

I saw some doctors sneak around and deliver babies at home, but there was a big fine and jail time for them if they were caught. Some compassionate doctors felt it was worth the risk, feeling there had to be someone to help babies arrive safely into this world.

Doctors weren't the only ones helping. I saw people taking care of each other. I was shown people who sacrificed material possessions and did good deeds for others. As midwives have done for thousands of years, there were trained people who knew how to assist with home births. It had to be secret, but they accepted this risk. Bartering was the only way to pay for their efforts.

There is hope and peace in knowing that even if we can't have our usual situations, there are alternatives to be found. When I saw something bad in the vision, there was always an answer somewhere, and someone who helped, even if it was not in the traditional way. There are those who were skilled, and who shared their skills with others. They knew what to do to help someone with a broken arm, a home birth, or whatever was needed. There is always an answer if we have faith.

I saw many miracles happen that illustrated this truth. In one miracle, I saw myself feeding family members as well as strangers. I opened a gallon-sized can of corn, and poured it into a four-gallon stockpot to make corn chowder.

My house was full of people walking, talking, and sitting. I looked through my kitchen and out of my dining room window to see tents, and even more people in my yard. These people were refugees from some event that wasn't made known to me. I just knew they were hungry.

I prayed while I made the soup. I told the Lord that I'd feed every hungry person who came to me if He would be kind enough to stretch the food. I just knew there would be enough.

I stood and ladled out soup. I sliced my homemade

bread, and I gave each person a slice with their corn chowder. They all ate in shifts, and someone washed the bowls as fast as they were used. Some families even brought their own dishes.

The people were courteous, and they waited until everyone had eaten before they came back for more. If they wanted seconds, they got seconds, and everyone got their fill.

I told people to spread the word that we had food to share. I poured soup into other pots, and sent them outside to feed those beyond my doors.

The soup never got low until I noticed there were only a few people left in line. It ran out just as the last person left the line. Three loaves of bread and four gallons of soup had fed hundreds of people. This was one of the many miracles I was shown that taught me to trust in God for help. He will help His people.

The vision continued, showing me that righteous people lived their lives as if the government was not there. This did not make the government happy, and they could see that these people were prospering, even though they had no money. So the government made laws that there couldn't be any trading, bartering, or exchanging of services or goods of any kind. There were also rewards given to those who caught people engaging in such activities.

I saw it was common for the government to want to control everything in the people's lives. The government made it very difficult to get anything. This was not the "land of the free" anymore. This was a land of sadness.

There was no middle class. The rich got richer, while the poor were undernourished and couldn't get the necessities of life. There were so many rules and regulations for food stamps that they were very hard to get. It seemed the people who needed them the most could never get them. Even things that were needed for bare survival were not allowed at times.

This was the way the evil leaders controlled the average citizens—by fear and deprivation. There were many government workers, and the government had control of everything, even the amount of food that was allowed per person. This rationing was also used to punish large families, and they would only be allowed enough food for a smaller family. There was a limit of people per household. So if there was a family of eight, but the limit was six, the family of eight would only be allowed enough food to feed six.

Divine intervention made the food stretch, and those with hope and faith had enough to feed their large families, and their children were not hungry. God always takes care of His children.

When I looked at the people I saw two groups. Some were walking around as usual, but I could see their spirits were asleep. They were not listening to God. It was kind of funny to see these people. It was as if they had two heads, a normal one that was upright, and a spirit one that was bent over with eyes closed.

Then there were those whose spirits were wide awake and knew what was going on. They waited for knowledge, inspiration, and direction from God. They sought to learn what to do, and how to help those who were spiritually asleep.

I also could see the beautiful brightness of these people. They were far brighter than the people who were asleep. I could see that they had the Light of Christ within them. It was distinct, and they shone like Jesus did. It was like they were in eternal happiness. Jesus loved them, and they loved Jesus.

They knew that God would open a way for them and help them, so they had no despair, and this was a great gift that the government couldn't take away from them.

It didn't matter which church they attended, it only mattered that they knew God, loved Him, and would follow Him even unto death. This was a rare thing to see, and gave them a brightness of spirit that was visible. When Jesus pointed out these people to me, He explained that it was the love inside of them, which shined so brightly that I could see it.

The government would imprison those who spoke up against them. If people knew of anyone who disagreed, there would be a reward for turning them in. This made it very difficult to have personal freedoms.

But even with all the adversity, these God-loving people knew that there was a way out, and that God would take care of them. They knew it didn't matter what happened to them, only that they were right with God, and did as He commanded. They had happiness in their homes, but for most people there was never a smile out in public. It was as though it was illegal to be happy. Most people's faces reflected fear, worry and depression.

I was also shown that the people who knew God had liberty with them, and were in safe havens. They were happy, and joyous. These people had dreams and visions, guiding them on what to do. As they prayed, I could see the light that came from their prayers, and it ascended to Heaven. This was wonderful, because when a prayer was said, I saw an angel sent specifically to carry out that request.

The faith in this group was great, and they knew that there was nothing essential that God would not provide. The faith in this group was so powerful that nothing could stop them. No high-tech detecting device the government could create was as powerful as the simple faith in that group. There were many in this faithful group, but to my sadness they were few in comparison to the millions who would not hear the promptings of Jesus.

The government knew that the God-fearing people existed, but the amazing thing was that no amount of technology could ever find them. Not even airplanes or heat-searching cameras could find them, for there was a cloak of protection over the Children of God. He made them safe. His power is greater than any oppressor.

I learned that even when evil is seemingly in control, that God is really in charge, and will help those who trust in Him through miracles, and divine guidance. His plans truly are greater than our dreams.

The vision shifted again and another possible scenario opened up.

MARTIAL LAW

I saw the United States' government had decided they were the police of the world. They would go into countries and do what they wanted without regard to that country's wishes. This made these countries angry, and in retaliation, America was invaded. Our armed forces were so busy in other lands that there was not enough protection on our own soil. The citizens' guns had been taken away, so there was no way families could defend themselves against the invaders.

I was saddened to see American citizens taken away to concentration camps. There was so much bloodshed that it ran down the streets. The invaders took great joy in killing children in front of their mothers' tearful eyes. Hunger and fear were everywhere.

There were those who were given direction from God to leave the cities and go to safe places that He led them to. I could see groups fleeing and following as the Spirit directed. I could see angels guarding them. They protected them with a whisper in an ear, or sometimes they would just point in the direction that the Heavens wanted them to go, and their leaders would go that way.

This was so comforting to me to see the Lord providing an escape from danger. There was a peace that I cannot describe, a peace that can only be found from Heaven.

When I was watching the Founding Fathers' lives, I could see the angels who were helping them make the choices that were needed to create the country we have today. This is what is happening in our day. There are people who can follow the Spirit's promptings and recognize the calling that God has given them. They know what needs to be done, and they will follow the Spirit and do it. I was shown that we can have God's help if we will ask Him for it. If we as a nation just seek God in a humble way we can have His direction, protection, and help.

I saw that people that followed God's promptings shared what they had, and there was not a lot of poor, because of this unselfishness among God's children.

I did not see a nation like it is now. Evil had taken over the country so deeply and completely in many ways, including the media. Most of the people were so wicked that the majority didn't want—or didn't know how—to have a God-centered life.

I saw that this country will never be the same, because of the evil doings of rich men, but we can have peace if we are a God-loving people. There is always hope in Christ. If we have hope God will provide for us as He did for the Children of Israel. In the end it doesn't matter what the government is doing, it only matters what we do, and if we are right with God.

Christopher Columbus had a vision of this great land, and the Holy Spirit prompted his journey that led to Europe's discovery of the New World. He once wrote: "I am a most noteworthy sinner, but I have cried out to the Lord for grace and mercy, and they have covered me completely. I have found the sweetest consolation since I made it my whole purpose to enjoy His marvelous Presence."[3]

The Pilgrims and others who were brought to this Land of Promise also knew it. Likewise, we also can know what our purpose is in regard to our nation.

God has a plan for us and for this country. I saw hope in this land, even after it was filled with wickedness. It will prosper and be great again. Our country was founded on liberty, and it will stay a land of liberty. If we stay with the right, and know that God is on our side, we will see good prevail, and evil will destroy evil. As it says in Psalms 145:20, "The Lord preserveth all them that love him; but all the wicked will he destroy."

There is a spirit of liberty—a freedom to live our lives as we choose—in all of us who love God. We all have that light. We just have to search for it within ourselves. It is part of our humanness, and what sets us apart from the beast. We humans feel, choose, and love, like no other creation on earth does. We are designed by God, and He gave us the right to feel liberty deep within our souls.

We all have to find our purpose, and why we are here. It is not always to be lived just for ourselves or our families, but also to help mankind. It only takes a few people to inspire others to find liberty, both for now, and in the future.

I ask all who read this book, to find that spirit of liberty within you, and help protect the freedoms that were given to us at such a great cost. We can't give up what Thomas Jefferson, George Washington, and others worked so hard to give to us. Let us remember what they have done for us.

Some people live without regard to their freedoms, and forget the future. Those who remember history know if freedom is not cherished, and if we don't respect the things that our forefathers did, our liberties could be lost.

We must all find that spirit of liberty within us, then and only then can we ever be free. You understand that we are only free, if in our hearts we are free. So in the end it truly is our choice; it is the lives we live that will determine if we have a free country with God in charge, or if we will allow ourselves to be in bondage. I say if we are free or not, it is up to us.

We can, one person at a time, change the outcome for millions. Pray and ask God to help you find the mission that has been placed within you. You will have to reach deep within yourself and find that strength you have, and I know it's there.

There are those who will not care to search for the spirit of liberty—and there were some with this attitude in 1776—but I encourage you to not give up just because some people don't understand. Who knows? It might be *you* that can change the hearts of other people. Understand that God has a plan for you. He has faith in humanity, and He has never lost hope in us.

Samuel Adams said, "I conceive that we cannot better express ourselves than by humbly supplicating the Supreme Ruler of the world that the rod of tyrants may be broken to pieces, and the oppressed made free again; that wars may cease in all the earth, and that the confusions that are and have been among nations may be overruled by promoting and speedily bringing on that holy and happy period when the kingdom of our Lord and Saviour Jesus Christ may be everywhere established, and all people everywhere willingly bow to the sceptre of Him who is Prince of Peace."[4]

So we have our lessons to learn, and my prayer is we learn them quickly before it is too late. We must follow the Savior, be unselfish, listen to the promptings God sends us, and stand up to protect our liberties.

I know that God is on our side. We can keep this land God's country so that the flag of freedom can fly until the Savior comes.

CHAPTER 12

Hope

I t's going to be so important, in the coming years, for us to keep hope in our hearts, and to understand that without hope we have nothing. Hope is the opposite of fear. Hope is the light we turn on in a room, and fear is the darkness that flees when we flick on the switch.

It's a natural human reaction to have fear, but hope is the faith we have in God, knowing that He will get us through. Without hope people despair, and when you despair, you give up. Hope means you can be happy even when things are going bad.

I agree with Lucy Maud Montgomery who said, "To despair is to turn your back on God."[1]

Entertaining fear invites illness, accidents, and troubles that we don't have to have. Fear attracts and acts as a conductor for problems, just as water is to electricity. No one would choose to put on a suit of armor and stand on a hill during a thunderstorm. You'd just be asking to get struck by a bolt of lightning.

If we use fear as a conductor, we will attract all kinds of fear-based events into our lives. If we have hope in the Lord, we will not fear. Faith can move mountains, so why wouldn't it help us as well? I was repeatedly taught this lesson, that we must hope, and not fear, no matter what comes to us in the future.

We must know that Christ is on our side, that He is willing and able to save us from anything. We must have complete trust in Him, because only through Him can we be saved. He said in John 14:27, "Let not your heart be troubled, neither let it be afraid."

I learned a truth about overcoming fear when we planned a camping trip near a lake. I kept feeling a nagging sense of dread and I didn't really want to go, but I had agreed to make a stop on the way to speak to a group of people. After camping, we would be going to a family reunion in Afton, Wyoming, organized to honor my great-great-grandfather who had helped settle that town.

For two days I packed and even hitched up the trailer by myself. I baked brownies, cookies, and turkey. I prepared all kinds of things to make it a fun time for my family. All the while I strongly felt that I didn't want to go, but every time I tried to get out of it I just couldn't.

I kept remembering that rivers are often near lakes, and I was concerned that there might be a stream by our campsite. I remember asking my mom if there was, and she told me that she didn't think so. I know the first thing my youngest boys, ages two and four, would want to do was to get into the water.

My heart sank as we pulled into the campground and I saw a deep, fast-moving river, the kind that swallows children and carries them away. The large snow-pack had melted, and what should have been a little stream was now a raging torrent.

I had been with twelve other people, most of them children, in my van for six hours. I was already exhausted, and I didn't want to spend my time chasing little boys away from dangerous water.

We set up camp, and I was careful to know where the youngest boys were at all times. After constantly admonishing them to stay away from the water, I let them throw rocks into a part that seemed to be shallow. They enjoyed it without realizing the danger such water could cause.

Always in my mind was the threat the water posed to my sons. I spent my days fretting about it and my nights worrying about it. If I couldn't see the boys as I did my chores, I would panic and start hunting for them. The effort was draining and time-consuming. I was always afraid they would fall in the river and be swept away.

After a couple days of this I had worried myself sick. That night I was intently praying for protection for my sons. I was surprised, and quite taken aback, when the answer I received was not the one I was seeking. I wanted guaranteed safety for my boys, and instead I was told to get rid of my fear. I didn't understand. Shouldn't I fear for my children's safety? Isn't that a maternal duty? So I prayed for understanding. I was told to still watch the boys, and to be concerned about their safety in a protective, maternal way, but not to be frantic, and panic. **I was told to let go of the fear.**

I decided to give my fear to God. I imagined all my fear was wrapped up in a little ball and I tossed it up to the Lord. I would be concerned and careful, but no longer fear.

I was reminded that the boys had special missions to do in life, and that it wasn't their time to die. I knew I still had to watch out for them, but I knew they'd be all right. I felt peace for the first time in days, and it was such a wonderful feeling. I started to enjoy the trip, and I relaxed. As Isaiah 12:2 says, "Behold, God is my salvation; I will trust, and not be afraid: for the Lord Jehovah is my strength and my song; He also is become my salvation."

I realized that this was a lesson I needed to learn. I had to keep fear out of my life. As I pondered over the events of this camping trip, and the meaning of symbolic rivers of fear in our daily lives, it was impressed upon me that this lesson was to prepare me for future times, soon to come.

In my experience in Heaven, I was shown the

events of the last days, and I knew that these events could be attracted by fear. I needed to practice keeping fear out of my life before those events came. I felt like the purpose of the camping trip was for me to learn this lesson. Now I felt actual peace. Until you get rid of fear there is no room for peace to be in you, and we must all start working on this now.

I learned another lesson about fear during my experience beyond the veil. In vision, I saw in the future a great illness that covered the country, and how fear could affect our health in the last days. Fear was the main cause of the illness that plagued the nation. I saw that if a person was afraid of getting sick—they got sick, but a person who didn't give in to the fear stayed well even if they were exposed to the illness.

The media falsely reported low death numbers for our area, and I knew they were higher because we had more funerals than reported deaths.

Most every house had several people who were ill. Our home was very rare in that we were all well. My family knew not to fear, and we took supplements and herbs to keep the illness away.

This disease was like the flu pandemic of 1918, a global disaster that killed more people than died in World War I. Stories were told of people dying overnight, or even in a few hours. Most victims were healthy young adults, instead of the old, young, and weak who are the usual victims of illness.

In recent years, the H1N1 virus emerged. It caused an overreaction of the body's immune system that made the immune system turn against the body, and destroy it. Healthy people who had a stronger immune system produced the fatal overreaction faster and more deadly. The illness I saw in our future was like this previous pandemic.

People in my town were so ill that they couldn't cook food for themselves. I saw myself taking food to a family who just had a death that had really hit them hard. Their grieving mother was very grateful for the food, but would only take it after I assured her that my family and I were well so we wouldn't infect them. They wouldn't even let me come into the house, for fear of contagion.

People in our town were taking every possible precaution against the illness, but I knew to not have fear, and to trust in the Lord. What the Lord had taught me beside the raging river had been a huge lesson to me. I could stand calmly beside the wild river with my children and be safe. I could live in a town stricken by disease and be at peace and protected. We were in the Lord's hands. I would trust Him and His will for our lives. I would not fear.

Another time I was taught about fear and God's ability to take care of us was when I saw in vision a sudden flood in the foothills that triggered a mudslide. This slide completely covered a subdivision of homes.

Just before it happened some people had been warned in dreams that they were to immediately leave their homes, and they did. They gathered their family and a few possessions before driving away to safety.

Houses were crushed under the oppressive weight of the mud and completely smothered. Some houses were carried away in splinters as the mudslide flowed over the neighborhood.

People found that air tunnels had miraculously formed in the deep mud, and they were able to use them to crawl out of their buried homes to safety. God had provided an escape for them too.

The final vision that taught me not to fear—and that the Lord would provide for us—was when I saw a tornado heading for my home. It was only about twenty feet away and would be upon us in seconds. Instantly I knew two things: I had to gather my children, and I had to pray. There was no time to run for a basement shelter. We needed God's immediate help.

We knelt in prayer and huddled in a circle. We pleaded for the Lord to intercede and protect us. Deep in my heart, I knew that if we continued to pray we would be safe.

We prayed with our eyes tightly closed and our heads bowed. I heard the wind howl and felt it whip my hair. It was so strong and loud I was sure my house was gone. I was praying only for my family's safety now. We kept our eyes shut, and continued to pray.

When the horrible noise stopped I looked around. To my relief and amazement my family was safe, our house was fine, and not even one window pane was broken. I was shocked that our house had not been destroyed by the fierce winds. I looked outside and saw that some houses nearby were totally destroyed, while others had been left untouched.

This is the important truth that I learned: there are, and will be times when we have nothing possible to save us except the Lord, and our faith in Him. Prayer is an answer to fear.

Fear is not from God, and He doesn't want us to fear. He can't help us if we are afraid. There is always hope when we believe in God. If we do not hope, fear will creep in and consume us. Hope gives us the strength to endure to the end, and obtain the rewards the Lord has promised to the faithful. **Hope will not be merely something nice to have, but will be absolutely necessary in our lives in these last days**.

As a flock of sheep is protected by the shepherd, we need not fear wolves, or danger. We should be careful, but not fear, because our Master is with us.

Religious leader Gordon Hinckley once said, "Our safety lies in the virtue of our lives. Our strength lies in our righteousness. God has made it clear that if we will not forsake Him, He will not forsake us."[2]

We need to learn to replace our natural fear instinct with hope and faith while trusting in the Lord. The more we ask God for His help to overcome fear, the easier it will be for us to react with difficulties with hope. It's something we need to make part of our souls, and not use it now and then. Remember that "Faith is not a pill you take, but a muscle you use."[3]

I find great comfort in a saying from the author of *Les Misérables*: "Have courage for the great sorrows of life, and patience for the small ones. And when you have laboriously accomplished your daily task, go to sleep in Peace. God is awake."[4]

When we think about the future, it can look frightening, but there are also many great things ahead for us. The great British leader Winston Churchill inspired people during the difficult times of World War II by saying, "Do not let us speak of darker days; let us rather speak of sterner days. These are not dark days: these are great days . . . and we must all thank God that we have been allowed, each of us according to our stations, to play a part in making these days memorable in the history of our race."[5]

God has helped many people survive during troubled times. Not only did He provide for their needs, He also sent His love as well. This account tells of a family who learned to leave their troubles in God's capable hands, and they were blessed with help, and peace:

World War II had been over for almost two years, but we were still on rations. It was February 1947, one of the hardest winters anyone could remember. Our home town of Bradford, Yorkshire, England, was the coldest spot in the nation, and it had snowed off and on for six weeks. By now the drifted snow was higher than our heads—that meant no cart could reach us to deliver our ration of coal. And we were running low.

There were six of us living together that winter—my husband and I, our two children, a young man who had been turned out of his own home when he joined the Church, and a woman whose daughter was serving a mission.

We did our best to keep warm, but we were almost out of fuel and we only had electricity at certain hours during the day. (Most of our power stations had been badly bombed during the war.)

It was Saturday when my husband went down to the cellar and carefully sifted the coal from the dust. All that remained was one shovelful of coal and a few cans of coal dust.

At church the next day, we received a shopping bag full of wood. The elders had sawed the wood from old railroad ties and stored it in the basement of the church. With this wood and our little pile of coal, we had fuel enough for one more day. That evening we knelt in prayer and asked the Lord to help us. As we prayed, our helplessness gave way to a sense of peace. When we went to bed, we felt content to leave the situation in the Lord's hands.

On Monday morning I put some wood, a can of dust, and the remaining coal into the fireplace. Then I waited until afternoon to start the fire—I wanted the house to be as warm as possible when the children got home from school. The fire lasted until nine or ten that night. We were amazed to discover that all six of us kept warm, and comfortable from the one little fire through the entire evening. My husband added a can of dust, and one log, but that was all.

The next morning I cleaned out the fireplace and began to lay paper and wood as I had the day before. Then I plucked up my courage and faith and went down to the cellar. Not knowing quite what to expect, I opened the door.

There, in the same corner where it had been yesterday, was a stack of coal that looked just like the coal we had burned the night before. I had the strangest feeling—had an angel brought it? I had no answer for my question, but I reverently scooped up the coal and took it upstairs.

How grateful we were that night for our miraculous fire. Our prayers were prayers of appreciation and praise.

The next morning when I went down to the cellar I found another stack of coal in the same corner. It was just enough. This miracle occurred every day that week until Saturday. By that time my husband felt that the snow had melted enough so that he would finally be *able to get us some coal. He took the children's sled, and as soon as he left I went down to the cellar. As soon as I saw the corner I knew that he would bring back some coal; there was no coal in the cellar. Later that day my husband brought back two lovely hundredweight sacks of coal.*

I still have no explanation for this incident. All I know is that it did happen and six of us witnessed it. And we know that God lives and answers prayers.[6]

God loves us and will lead us through whatever is ahead of us. He has promised us rest, and joy. Is this not something to hope for?

I believe the miracle that happened during Old Testament times to the prophet Elijah can happen in our day as well. In 1st Kings 17:10-16 we read:

So he arose and went to Zarephath. And when he came to the gate of the city, behold, the widow woman was there gathering of sticks: and he called to her, and said, Fetch me, I pray thee, a little water in a vessel, that I may drink.

And as she was going to fetch it, he called to her, and said, Bring me, I pray thee, a morsel of bread in thine hand.

And she said, As the Lord thy God liveth, I have not a cake, but an handful of meal in a barrel, and a little oil in a cruse: and, behold, I am gathering two sticks, that I may go in and dress it for me and my son, that we may eat it, and die.

And Elijah said unto her, Fear not; go and do as thou hast said: but make me thereof a little cake first, and bring it unto me, and after make for thee and for thy son.

For thus saith the Lord God of Israel, The barrel of meal shall not waste, neither shall the cruse of oil fail, until the day that the Lord sendeth rain upon the earth.

And she went and did according to the saying of Elijah: and she, and he, and her house, did eat [many] days.

And the barrel of meal wasted not, neither did the cruse of oil fail, according to the word of the Lord, which he spake by Elijah."

The cruse of oil didn't run out and the barrel of meal was not wasted. The woman had the faith to give the last of her food to feed this man, and she was blessed for it. I know that this will happen again as we trust in God.

CHAPTER 13

The Spirit of Liberty

Inscribed upon the Liberty Bell is this scripture from Leviticus 25:10: "Proclaim liberty throughout all the land unto all the inhabitants thereof."

Liberty! Such a sweet word! God-given, hard-won, and thanks to the Founding Fathers it isn't a word that we can only dream about, it's our reality.

I treasure my visit with the Founding Fathers, and with all of the Patriots who sacrificed so much for us. It was a privilege to get to know them and to be taught by them. I'm also glad I got to journey in their footsteps and see how they lived.

I have developed a great love and appreciation for these extraordinary people. These feelings of love and respect will stay in my heart forever. I cannot convey my feelings of gratitude for all they have done for us and our country. The privileges we enjoy today are a direct result of their life's work. They took the spirit of liberty, and with God's guidance, created a glorious nation with far-reaching effects. When I think of all the patriots who worked and fought for our freedoms, I am reminded of an early hymn:

Oh beautiful for heroes proved in liberating strife,
Who more than self, their country loved,
And mercy more than life!
America! America! May God thy gold refine,
Till all success be nobleness,
And ev'ry gain divine! [1]

I pray that we can also find the Spirit of Liberty in our hearts and treasure what the Founding Fathers did for us. I hope that we will never let our freedoms slip away from us, and that we will know the importance of liberty in our lives, and our posterity's lives.

I hope we remember the Founding Fathers' message for us to keep God in our country and our personal lives. If so, we can continue to have His help and liberty in our nation. Without liberty, we would no longer have the America that our Founding Fathers helped to create. Benjamin Franklin summed it up when he said, "Where liberty dwells, there is my country."[2]

As we discover the Spirit of Liberty within ourselves, it is essential that we share this light with those around us. As we go through life, there are a few things that we can do to help one another. They are simple and sometimes not really meant to be known about, like a secret little present left at a doorstep. Or paying the check for the person in line behind you in a restaurant.

It starts within us, its then we can give it like a gift to others. It is also contiguous. It can also be compared to laughter—when it starts, it catches on and can't be stopped.

Sometimes it has to be taught that we all have the right to have liberty. It isn't a right given to only a few. Should we sit back and say, "I am only one person. What can I do?" No! It starts with one person who teaches another, and so on and so on.

If only we can understand one person can make a difference, there would not be a tyrannical government because the people would not let it happen. Are we like the frog that is cooked alive because we don't realize that we are being cooked? If we truly knew the power we hold—the power we know God gave us—there wouldn't be anything a government could do to us.

It only took a few patriots to change a country in 1776. It took a young maiden in France to help people realize that they didn't want to be conquered by England.

There doesn't have to be a war. Instead, it can be quiet, it can be as the morning sun peering over the horizon slowly and soon it is as the noon day in brightness. The light can't be hidden and it can't be blocked. This is the light of Christ within us. It's there for all of us. It might be deeper in some people than others, but it's there.

I have faith in Christ that the light will shine and

come forth. It will be like a line of candles when one is lit and is placed close to another so the flame will light the next one. Then that flame will continue to light the next and the next until there are so many candles that the light can't be extinguished by any power known to mankind. This can only done by the love that God gave us—the pure love of Christ.

The saying "Love Conquers All" is true. Love is the light of Christ. If we love Christ we will spread His love far and wide. We never know how we can touch another person by giving them hope. This is the secret. So please spread this light that is within you and then pass it on to others around you.

It is my hope and prayer that we all can find the light that is within all of us. I know that Jesus wants us to teach others to find it as well. I know He is the cornerstone of truth and that through Him all truth is told. He is always guiding those who will listen and who have the knowledge and the desire to hear to the quiet whisperings of the Holy Spirit.

I know that there are special angels sent to us. They might be in the flesh or be heavenly visitors that will help us until that glorious day when Jesus comes again. I want to live my life so I can see Him again. My hope and prayer is that this book brings you peace, power, and knowledge to find the spirit of liberty within you. The future is bright and beautiful. Have no fear. There is no end. There is only a new beginning!

George Washington's Vision at Valley Forge

This vision was told to a reporter named Wesley Bradshaw by Anthony Sherman, an officer who served under General Washington at Valley Forge. In the vision, Washington sees three great trials overtake the Union. These were the Revolutionary War, the Civil War, and the greatest threat, a war fought on the soil of the United States near the time of Jesus' return to reign on the earth.

For many years copies of Washington's vision at Valley Forge have been in existence. This version is a reprint of a newspaper article first published in the *National Tribune* in 1859.

Here is Wesley Bradshaw's explanation about the recording of the vision:

"The last time I ever saw Anthony Sherman was

on the Fourth of July, 1859, in Independence Square. He was then ninety-nine years old, and becoming very feeble. But though so old, his dimming eyes rekindled as he gazed upon Independence Hall, which he came to visit once more. 'Let us go into the hall,' he said. 'I want to tell you of an incident of Washington's life— one which no one alive knows of except myself; and if you live, you will before long see it verified.

"'From the very opening of the Revolution we experienced all phases of fortune, now good and now ill, one time victorious and another conquered. The darkest period we had, I think, was when Washington, after several reverses, retreated to Valley Forge, where he resolved to spend the winter of 1777. Ah! I have often seen the tears coursing down our dear commander's care-worn cheeks, as he would be conversing with a confidential officer about the condition of his poor soldiers. You have doubtless heard the story of Washington's going into the thicket to pray. Well, it was not only true, but he used often to pray in secret for aid and comfort from God, the interposition of whose Divine Providence brought us safely through the darkest days of tribulation.

"'One day, I remember it well, the chilly winds whistled through the leafless trees, though the sky was cloudless and the sun shone brightly, he remained in his quarters nearly all the afternoon alone. When he came out, I noticed that his face was a shade paler than usual, and there seemed to be something on his mind of more than ordinary importance. Returning just after dusk, he dispatched an orderly to the quarters of the officer I mention, who was presently in attendance. After a preliminary conversation of about half an hour, Washington, gazing upon his companion with that strange look of dignity which he alone could command, said to the latter:

WASHINGTON'S VISION

"I do not know whether it is owing to the anxiety of my mind, or what, but this afternoon, as I was sitting at this table engaged in preparing a dispatch, something seemed to disturb me. Looking up, I beheld standing opposite me a singularly beautiful female. So astonished was I, for I had given strict orders not to be disturbed, that it was some moments before I found language to inquire into the cause of her presence. A second, a third, and even a fourth time did I repeat my question, but received no answer from my mysterious visitor except a slight raising of her eyes.

"By this time I felt strange sentiments spreading through me. I would have risen, but the riveted gaze of the being before me rendered volition impossible. I assayed once more to address her, but my tongue had become useless, even thought itself had become paralyzed. A new influence, mysterious, potent, irresistible, took possession of me. All I could do was to gaze steadily, vacantly at my unknown visitor. Gradually, the surrounding atmosphere seemed as though becoming filled with sensations and luminous. Everything about me seemed to rarify, the mysterious visitor herself becoming more airy, and yet more distinct to my sight than before. I now began to feel as one dying, or rather to experience the sensations which I have sometimes imagined accompany dissolution. I did not think, I did not reason, I did not move; all were alike impossible. I was only conscious of gazing fixedly, vacantly at my companion.

"Presently I heard a voice saying, 'Son of the Republic, look and learn,' while at the same time my visitor extended her arm eastwardly. I now beheld a heavy white vapor at some distance rising fold upon fold. This gradually dissipated, and I looked upon a strange scene. Before me lay spread out in one vast plain all the countries of the world—Europe, Asia, Africa, and America. I saw rolling and tossing between Europe and America the billows of the Atlantic, and between Asia and America lay the Pacific. 'Son of the Republic,' said the same mysterious voice as before, 'look and learn.'

"At that moment I beheld a dark, shadowy being, like an angel floating in mid-air, between Europe and America, dipping water out of the ocean in the hollow of each hand. He sprinkled some upon America with his right hand, while with his left hand he cast some on Europe. Immediately a dark cloud raised from these countries and joined in mid-ocean. For a while it remained stationary, and then moved slowly westward, until it enveloped America in its murky folds. Sharp flashes of lightning passed through it at intervals, and I heard the smothered groans and cries of the American people.

"A second time the angel dipped water from the ocean, and sprinkled it out as before. The dark cloud was then drawn back to the ocean, in whose heaving billows it sank from view. A third time I heard the mysterious voice saying, 'Son of the Republic, look and learn.' I cast my eyes upon America and beheld villages and towns and cities springing up one after another until the whole land from the Atlantic to the Pacific was dotted with them. Again I heard the mysterious voice say, 'Son of the Republic, the end of the century cometh, look and learn.'

"At this the dark, shadowy angel turned his face southward, and from Africa I saw an ill-omened spectre approach our land. It flitted slowly over every town and city. The inhabitants presently set themselves in battle array against each other. As I continued looking, I saw a bright angel, on whose brow rested a crown of light, on which was traced the word 'Union,' bearing the American flag, which he placed between the divided nation, and said, 'Remember ye are brethren.' Instantly the inhabitants, casting from them their weapons, became friends once more and united around the National Standard.

"And again I heard the mysterious voice saying, 'Son of the Republic, look and learn.' At this the dark, shadowy angel placed a trumpet to his mouth and blew three distinct blasts; and taking water from the ocean, he sprinkled it upon Europe, Asia, and Africa. Then my eyes beheld a fearful scene: from each of these countries arose thick, black clouds that were joined into one. And throughout this mass there gleamed a dark red light by which I saw hordes of armed men, who, moving with the cloud, marched by land and sailed by sea to America, which country was enveloped in the volume of the cloud. And I dimly saw these vast armies devastate the whole country and burn the villages, towns, and cities that I beheld were springing up.

"As my ears listened to the thundering of the cannon, clashing of swords, and the shouts and cries of millions in mortal combat, I heard again the mysterious voice saying, 'Son of the Republic, look and learn.' When the voice had ceased, the dark, shadowy angel placed his trumpet once more to his mouth and blew a long and fearful blast.

"Instantly a light as of a thousand suns shone down from above me, and pierced and broke into fragments the dark cloud which enveloped America. At the same moment the angel, upon whose head still shone the word 'Union', and who bore our national flag in one hand and a sword in the other, descended from the Heavens, attended by legions of white spirits. These immediately joined the inhabitants of America, who I perceived were well-nigh overcome, but who immediately taking courage again, closed up their broken ranks and renewed the battle. Again, amid the fearful noise of the conflict, I heard the mysterious voice saying, 'Son of the Republic, look and learn.' As the voice ceased, the shadowy angel for the last time dipped water from the ocean and sprinkled it upon America. Instantly the dark cloud rolled back, together with the armies it had brought, leaving the inhabitants of the land victorious.

"Then once more I beheld the villages, towns, and cities springing up where I had seen them before, while the bright angel, planting the azure standard he had brought in the midst of them, cried with a loud voice, 'While the stars remain, and the Heavens send down dew upon the earth, so long shall the Union last.' And taking from his brow the crown on which was blazoned the word 'Union', he placed it upon the Standard, while the people, kneeling down, said, 'Amen.'

"The scene instantly began to fade and dissolve, and I at last saw nothing but the rising, curling vapor I at first beheld. This also disappearing, I found myself once more gazing upon the mysterious visitor, who, in the same voice I had heard before, said, 'Son of the

Republic, what you have seen is thus interpreted: Three great perils will come upon the Republic. The most fearful is the third, passing which the whole world united shall not prevail against her. Let every child of the Republic learn to live for his God, his land, and the Union.' With these words the vision vanished, and I started from my seat, and felt that I had seen a vision wherein had been shown me the birth, progress, and destiny of the United States."

"Such, my friends," concluded the venerable narrator, "were the words I heard from General Washington's own lips, and America will do well to profit by them."

SOURCES

The weblinks listed below were functioning at the time of publication.

Introduction

1. http://www.revolutionary-war-and-beyond.com/quotes-by-benjamin-franklin.html
2. http://www.brainyquote.com/quotes/keywords/liberty.html

Chapter 2

1. http://florida.republicanassembly.org/2011/09/19/americas-founding-mothers/
2. http://quotes.liberty-tree.ca/quotes/god
3. http://thinkexist.com/quotation/bad_men_cannot_make_good_citizens-it_is/154033.html
4. http://thinkexist.com/quotation/bad_men_cannot_make_good_citizens-it_is/154033.html
5. http://thinkexist.com/quotation/the_longer_i_live-the_more_convincing_proofs_i/261270.html
6. http://www.sourcedquotes.com/John-Adams-quote-on-liberty-posterity-you-will-never-know
7. http://www.quotationspage.com/quote/4949.html

Chapter 3

1. General George Washington's Angelic Visitation at Valley Forge and the Vision of the Future of the United States. (See Appendix.)

2.   "Shot heard 'round the world", *Concord Hymn*, 1837, Ralph Waldo Emerson.

Chapter 4

1.   http://www.whitehouse.gov/about/presidents/ thomasjefferson
2.   Letter to Peter Carr, his nephew, August 19, 1785. http:// avalon.law.yale.edu/18th_century/let31.asp

Chapter 5

1.   http://www.marksquotes.com/Founding-Fathers/ Jefferson/
2.   *Hey America, Your Roots are Showing*, Megan Smolenyak2, Citadel Press Books, Kensington Publishing Corp. New York, NY, 2012, Page 126.
3.   General George Washington's Angelic Visitation at Valley Forge and the Vision of the Future of the United States. (See Appendix.)

Chapter 6

1.   http://site.heritage.org/research/features/almanac/ madison.html
2.   http://www.brainyquote.com/quotes/quotes/j/ jamesmadis392906.html

Chapter 7

1.   http://www.revolutionary-war-and-beyond.com/ benjamin-franklin-quotations.html

Chapter 8

1. http://www.joan-of-arc.us/
2. http://www.maidofheaven.com/joanofarc_quotes_autobiography.asp
3. http://www.maidofheaven.com/joanofarc_quotes_autobiography.asp
4. http://thinkexist.com/quotes/joan_of_arc/
5. http://www.maidofheaven.com/joanofarc_quotes_autobiography.asp
6. http://thinkexist.com/quotes/joan_of_arc/
7. http://www.maidofheaven.com/joanofarc_quotes_autobiography.asp

Chapter 9

1. Hannah Withrop. http://florida.republicanassembly.org/2011/09/19/americas-founding-mothers/
2. http://florida.republicanassembly.org/2011/09/19/americas-founding-mothers/
3. http://ehcnc.org/history/penelopebarker.php
4. William Ross Wallace, "For the hand that rocks the cradle—is the hand that rules the world." http://thinkexist.com/quotation/for_the_hand_that_rocks_the_cradle-is_the_hand/165109.html
5. Wiz Khalifa, " A man who treats his woman like a princess is proof that he has been raised by a queen." http://www.searchquotes.com/quotation/A_man_who_treats_his_woman_like_a_princess_is_proof_that_he_has_been_raised_by_a_queen./327689/

6. http://www.brainyquote.com/quotes/authors/d/dolley_madison.html

7. http://www.brainyquote.com/quotes/authors/m/martha_washington.html

Chapter 10

1. http://www.constitutionfacts.com/?section=foundingFathers&page=fascinatingFacts.cfm

2. http://www2.vcdh.virginia.edu/lewisandclark/biddle/biographies_html/jefferson.html

Chapter 11

1. Chuck Baldwin http://www.cancertutor.com/Quotes/Quotes_Patriotic.html

2. http://www.brainyquote.com/quotes/quotes/m/margaretme100502.html

3. http://www.brainyquote.com/quotes/authors/c/christopher_columbus.html

4. http://ringthebellsoffreedom.com/Quotes/sadamscontent.htm

Chapter 12

1. *Anne of Green Gables*, Lucy Maud Montgomery, New York: Bantam Books, 1998.

2. Religious Leader, Gordon B. Hinckley, October Conference 2001, *Till We Meet Again*.

3. Unknown Author.

4. *Les Misérables*, Hugo, Victor, 1802-1885. New York, NY: Fawcett Premier, 1961.

5. Sir Winston Churchill, Speech given at Harrow School, 29 October 1941.

6. Marjorie A. McCormick, *"One Shovelful of Coal,"* Ensign Magazine, Oct. 1979, 49–50.

Chapter 13

1. America the Beautiful, Katharine Lee Bates, 1917, third verse.

2. http://www.americanrevival.org/quotes/forefathers.htm

ABOUT THE AUTHOR

Suzanne Freeman lives in a small town in the Western United States with her husband James and their children. She loves to cook and sew, and she uses these talents to bless the lives of those around her.

Suzanne is available for public speaking events. Reimbursement for travel expenses is appreciated.

You can contact Suzanne through her publisher at: public_relations@springcreekbooks.com.